Listen to Me

*A Book for Women and Men
About Father–Son Relationships*

Gerald G. Jampolsky, M.D.
and
Lee L. Jampolsky, Ph.D.

Celestial Arts
Berkeley, California

Cover design by Catherine E. Campaigne
Text design by FORM FOLLOWS FUNCTION

FIRST PRINTING 1996

Library of Congress Cataloging-in-Publication Data

Jampolsky, Gerald G., 1925–
    Listen to me : a book for women and men about father–son
relationships / Gerald G. Jampolsky and Lee L. Jampolsky.
        p.   cm.
    Includes bibliographical references.
    ISBN 0-89087-810-2
    1. Fathers—United States.   2. Fatherhood—Psychological
aspects.   3. Fathers and sons—United States.   I. Jampolsky,
Lee L., 1957–.   II. Title.
HQ756.J3594   1996
306.874'2—dc20   96-13861
                                                          CIP

 ·   2   3   4   5   6   7   8   9   0   /   00   99   98

Table of Contents

We dedicate this book with boundless love and appreciation for all the lessons we learned from Leo Jampolsky, Jerry's dad and Lee's grandfather, and to Vern Powell, Lee's maternal grandfather.

We also dedicate this book to all the fathers and sons and the women in their lives who have come to our workshops and shared so intimately and taught us so much.

We wish to express our deepest gratitude and appreciation to our agent, Joe Durepos, for the many hours he spent guiding and helping us with every aspect of this book. Without his help this book would never had reached fruition.

We also want to express our gratitude to David Hinds of Celestial Arts for believing in this book.

The image of my father floats like a specter
as I try to form my thoughts about manhood.

KENT NERBURN, *LETTERS TO MY SON*

A father is someone who knows you are not perfect
but treats you as if you were.

ANONYMOUS

Foreword

by Hal Zina Bennett, Ph.D.

How little we know about our fathers—and our sons! It is a sad commentary on our society that even in the best of families, there is so often a barrier between father and son. It is a barrier separating men from each other and from the women in their lives. As a young man, there were so many times I blamed my own father for what I felt were his shortcomings. Whenever I perceived something lacking in my own make-up, I'm afraid Dad was a fair target. I now know that the tension between us affected everyone in our family. It particularly pained my mother, who wanted more than anything for my Dad and me to be at peace. Years later, I had my own son and stepsons. By the time they were all grown and I had struggled with my own successes and failures as a father, I learned the meaning of forgiveness toward my own father.

I don't know what is responsible for the distance that grows between sons and fathers, from the time we hold our infant sons in our arms and the time they become men. *Listen to Me* narrows this distance and can show men another way of being. Of equal importance, it reveals to wives, mothers, and daughters some of the secrets we men rarely even tell ourselves. The work of the Jampolskys is an important breakthrough. There is no other way to describe this courageous and moving book. I believe it will can create a healing bridge not only between fathers and sons but between all men and women.

Having known Jerry for many years as his editor and friend, I have not been a stranger to the tensions between him and his sons. It was never the tension that we read in magazine articles about how so and so's famous father (or mother) beat them or abused them sexually. It was more a tension that is so common in contemporary families that it almost, but not quite, slips by unnoticed. It's "normal." But for Lee and Jerry, both of whom have been on spiritual paths for much of their adult years, normal just wasn't good enough. They both knew there were aspects of their relationship they wanted to improve.

I remember Jerry and Lee first talking about this book five years ago before they actually sat down to write it. They both circled around it, moving toward it, and then away. It was clear to me as their friend that the idea of committing themselves to the project both attracted and repelled them. Writing a book wasn't what was bothering them, of course. Neither father nor son were strangers to the task; combined they had twelve books in print. No, the challenge reached far deeper than writing—they had to confront each other, as well as themselves, as honestly and openly as they could. Each had to confront their own illusions about themselves and the other person: *Was I really as loving and caring as I could have been toward my children when they were growing up? In what ways could I have better supported my wife, that would have made both her and my son's lives easier? Am I being fair in judging my father as I've been doing all these years? Could I have been more supportive during the difficult times? How might I have made our good times together more meaningful? How could I, as a teenager or young man, have made*

my father's life a little easier? And most of all, *Why is it so difficult to look him in the eye and say with all my heart, I love
you?*

After considerable debate, and following months and
months of the most creative procrastination I've ever witnessed, Lee and Jerry decided that the most straight-forward
way to write the book would be through an exchange of letters. In these letters, we are taken right into the hearts and
minds of the authors. The story they tell is one that will move
every man and woman. There is a wisdom here that can bring
all of us closer to the lives we want for ourselves and our
loved ones. By sharing the authors doubt, anger, frustration,
and genuine affection for each other, we enter a place of compassion and understanding that is rare in any book. The letters help us heal within ourselves the separation we may feel
in our own father–son relationships.

These letters between Lee and Jerry reveal deeply felt
bonds, anxieties, self-doubts, and wounds that are part of
every man's life. They are the source of tension and concern
shared by anyone who is close to them, regardless of gender.
Yet, because we men are so indoctrinated with the idea that
we must never reveal these to the outside world for fear of
showing weakness, our vulnerability also remains a mystery
for our wives, sisters, mothers, and daughters. For women
reading this book, I am certain that the writing will open
doors they never imagined possible. And hopefully, these
openings will help all of us take a giant step toward better
communication between the sexes, as well as between adults
and children.

The gift these authors offer us is a vehicle for the heart
and mind to move beyond the stereotypes of being male in
the modern world. The teachings here come so unexpect-
edly that the reader is taken off guard and given a glimpse

of another way of looking at the world. In the moments when the boundaries between Jerry and Lee are dissolved, we experience our own boundaries shifting and dissolving. We go beyond the limits we have placed upon ourselves and begin to feel how it might be to find peace of mind in our own parental relationships.

There were many times in reading these pages that I grew impatient with either Jerry's or Lee's stubbornness; but then a few pages later, I discovered it was my own bullheadedness that troubled me. And there were times when I said to myself, How can he be so shortsighted! Why can't he just let go and let in the love and the caring that's there for both of them? Then I was reminded that they were only mirroring my own feelings about my life and the interweaving of my relationship with my dad, one that I often wished could be better. In moments such as these, I realized that this is where our courage counts the most, for the authors keep going until the conflicts fade and the light shines through. Unlike so many of us, they persist. They face their differences, let each other have their own private truths, and finally manage to touch that point where they are teachers to each other, at last embracing with forgiveness and a deeper understanding of their own lives.

If this book works the way I think it can, women who read it will feel closer to the men in their lives, and men will feel a little closer, and a little more open with each other. There is a tenderness here but also the kind of toughness without which we can never enjoy true understanding and love.

This is an important book, not just because it offers a better understanding of the father–son relationship, but because it opens up new avenues for dialogue and, ultimately, healing between men and women.

Authors' Introduction

Lee

I wanted not to write this book more than I wanted to. My friend and agent, Joe Durepos, encouraged me to consider how helpful and powerful it could be—even more powerful if I could write it with my father. Despite his encouragement there seemed to be two voices in my mind. One said "Lee, don't be crazy. Your relationship with your father is good enough. You get along with him now. Don't upset what you've got." This voice hid the fears that took a long time to uncover. One large fear was that I had so much hidden rage that releasing it would destroy my life. A calmer voice persisted. "Further healing of your relationship with your father will open your heart and free you." This voice quietly endured, drawing me beyond my fears.

I undertake this project because I want to be alive and no longer just live. "Good enough" isn't good enough when it comes to intimacy and healing. My ability to experience love is limited only by the doors that I choose to keep shut. Our relationships with our fathers can be doorways to love, forgiveness,* and intimacy, or they can be cages that keep us trapped in judgment, shame, and anger.

---

*As we use the term, forgiveness does not mean saying to a person who has hurt us, "Oh, forget about it. It doesn't matter." Rather, it has to do with releasing ourselves from the past. We'll discuss this in detail in chapter nine.

My parents were married until I was fifteen years old. My mother, Pat, spent a great deal of time with my older brother Greg and I in our early years. Mom was also a very creative person and worked hard in her profession as an interior designer. Dad was a psychiatrist and had an excellent name in the small community of Tiburon where we lived. Greg was always doing well in athletics and I was competing on the horse show circuit. From the outside, we were the model family. Yet inside I felt a tension just beneath the surface of the family, but it was never talked about. This lack of peace was combined with a deficit of feeling good about myself.

Despite many workshops, therapy, and classes on psychology and spiritual development, I never really began to heal this inner turmoil until addressing my relationship with my father. Opening the door to feelings about my dad also opened the door to how I was and am in relationships with others, most notably women.

I am currently married to Carny. This is my second marriage. I feel a deep commitment to Carny, though we have had our challenges, many of which I share in this book. My first marriage was to Amanda when we were in our twenties. It lasted only six months, despite the fact that Amanda was also a wonderful woman.

When I began looking deeply at my relationship with my father, I saw that many of my difficulties with intimacy with women were traceable to not seeing my mother and father really relating with any depth. I saw both my parents as feeling trapped and largely coexisting. Other than talking over nightly cocktails, I saw very little genuine communication between them. When as an adult I tried to have emotional intimacy with a woman, I became a confused and wounded little boy. Healing my relationship with my father is a central part to being a whole man who is available to have intimacy with a woman.

Most everything I have said I also believe is true about father–daughter relationships. With both Carny and Amanda I can now see how much our fathers' influences affected our relationships. Any time one or both of the partners has an unhealed relationship with their father, there is destined to be some problems. This is not bad news, for once we see this we can begin to put our energy into healing the wounds. As long as we remain blind to the affects of our relationships with our fathers, we can never have a successful relationship.

Though both of my parents were college educated and intelligent, I felt that the role of my mother was supposed to be one of supporter. The covert message I received was that Mom could work but Dad's work was more important. On the surface they were equals but the real message was that Mom should be just slightly in the background.

This is not to say that my mother was a passive, subservient woman. Mom found ways to have power in the relationship. Most of the time I saw my father as trying to please her without ever having a sense of himself. My dad was a curious mix of both pleaser and controller.

As much as I hated to see or admit it, I adopted many of the same dynamics as my parents in how I related to both Amanda and Carny. Until I really looked at what Dad covertly taught me about relating to women, I just repeated his patterns. I was with bright, attractive, sensitive women that in my mind and heart I saw as equals. But inside me was my family history and this prevailed. I always supported the women I was involved with in what they did, though I had a secret feeling that my activities were more important. I ended up in the role of trying to please at all costs, often at the loss of my sense of identity. At the same time, like my father, I also tried to control. Under such circumstances I had no more chance of a successful and intimate relationship than my parents did.

During years of therapy as a client, and thousands of hours in the role of therapist, I avoided seeing the fundamental importance of the father–son relationship. Our culture and psychology supported my oversight, with the emphasis and importance traditionally placed on relationships with our mothers. As I write this, I glance over to my wife's desk and see the magazine *Mothering*. A familiar tug pulls at me. What about fathering? Where were the articles and magazines to help me be a father and honor the role of fatherhood?

Only recently have a few books and articles appeared about fathers and their wounds. Reading them has helped me to know that I am not alone in my feelings. Still, much of what I have read overlooks something I feel to be integral to healing. All too many of the writings fail to fully address the spiritual aspect of being.

Something quite unexpected and remarkable happened as I began to heal my relationship with my father: I found healing in my relationship with God. Many of the feelings I had with my father also separated me from God. I was angry with my father but did not want to admit it. I judged my father and held on to what I thought he did wrong, especially things that I felt were unjust. I feared that I would never live up to my father's expectations and vacillated between giving up and trying to be perfect. I loved my father but did not know how to express the love. Curiously, I never made the connection that my yearnings for a deeper relationship with my father had anything to do with my yearnings for a deeper connection with God.

My hopes for this book are to say to my father: "You are important. You are so important that I can't live fully without healing the wounds of our past." I want to say to myself: "Being a father is the single most important process that you will ever undertake. Until you heal your relationship with your father, your daughters will never fully know the father you can be."

Jerry

When Lee came to me two years ago to talk about the possibilities of writing a book about fathers and sons, I was elated and thrilled. I thought it would be a wonderful experience to write a book with my son.

As time passed, I began to have second thoughts. Like Lee, I wondered if I really wanted to challenge our relationship when we seemed closer than either of us had thought was possible. I remembered times when our relationship had become so tense and difficult that it seemed we would never be able to break through the barriers that kept us apart.

Part of me didn't want to take any risks on our relationship. I was frightened of facing the pains of the past with my son. Did I really want to reveal the secrets that remained hidden even from myself?

As we began to discuss our past together in preparation for writing this book, some of the memories that surfaced were agonizing to look at. It was as though they were buried deep inside me, thorns that I knew I had to pull out.

It took almost a year before both of us made the commitment to write this book. I do believe that each of us needed this experience to further our own healing. There were times when we both hesitated, wondering if we were really safe to let each other, or anyone else, know so much about our inner, secret selves.

Although we had both written books before, Lee had never written a book with another person, let alone with his father. I had written four books with my wife, Diane Cirincione, and knew from personal experience how challenging a writing partnership can be.

In writing this book Lee and I found that sharing our vulnerability has been an important part of our healing process. It has allowed us to get to know each other on a much deeper level. It has also created an atmosphere where love and intimacy allow us to welcome others to see us as we really are.

Lee knew my parents and over the years I had shared with him many of my early childhood experiences. But I don't think I ever sat down and gave him any kind of sequential history.

I remember being an extremely shy child who was filled with fear, wondering what awful things were going to occur next. Having dyslexia and being unable to learn to read added to my burdens.

My father, Leo, was born in a small town near Odessa, Russia. As I understand it, his family were poor farmers. My dad came to the United States to avoid going into the army when he was 16 years old. My mother, Tillie, was born in Manchester, England (her parents were born in Russia) and came to the United States when she was a teenager. They met while working in a department store in Brooklyn, New York.

When I was born February 11, 1925 in Long Beach, California my dad sold fruit to markets. Later he and my mom opened their own dried fruit store. My parents were extremely strict and controlling. You didn't dare get out of line. We boys did as we were told and didn't dare express our feelings. I grew up afraid to express my feelings.

I had two older brothers. Les, nine years older than me,

became a chemist, and Art, six years older, became an ophthalmologist. By the time I was 12 years old, both brothers were away in college, and I became the only child. The age difference between my brothers and me did not allow for a close relationship. As time went on, my brothers tended to act like my father figures.

In my memory, which is filled with many holes, my mother made all the decisions. I saw my dad as passive and weak. Although there were times he would become assertive, he always seemed to give in to my mother. They argued constantly. As a teenager I remember wondering why they stayed married to each other. To me it was one of those relationships where they could not live with or without each other.

I learned from my dad that women are dangerous, unpredictable, and strong, capable of rejecting, hurting, and abandoning you at a moment's notice. I learned that a woman was someone that you could not trust and someone with whom you had to repress your real feelings. (My paternal grandmother was extremely strong and played the domineering role in the family.)

My first marriage was with Pat. She was a strong woman who could easily be emotionally volatile in our relationship, just like my mother. I projected a lot of my unresolved conflicts and fears regarding women onto Pat. Pat became like a screen in a movie theater, upon whom I projected all those old conflicts.

My fear of being abandoned by women persisted after our 20-year marriage broke up. I continued to be attracted to strong women and fearful that I would be abandoned. I can see now that I used to do many things to provoke those feelings about abandonment. I continued to be fearful to have intimate deep conversations and kept my own inner life a secret for fear I would be rejected again.

My relationship with my present wife, Diane, is the most intimate and honest relationship I have ever had with anyone. It is built on trust, intimacy, and equality where our relationship with God comes first. To get to this place I had to go back and resolve some of my unfinished business with my parents and misperceived ideas about women. At the beginning of our relationship, there were plenty of abandonment fears. Initially I was afraid that the 21-year difference in our ages would lead to being abandoned once again; I was also afraid that if Diane really knew what I was like inside she would want no part of me. I feel blessed and most happy to say that I was wrong.

Before writing this book I was convinced that my relationship with my father was completely healed. My father died in 1982 at age 94. At the time of his death I really thought I felt complete with him. One of the benefits of writing this book with Lee was recognizing that not only was there more work to do with Lee but also with my father. I needed to learn that I could complete the process with my father even though he is no longer here to communicate with me.

Writing this book has been an amazing process for me. It has been a kaleidoscope of pain, joy, agony, and bliss. It has resulted in a more tender, gentle, intimate, and loving father and son relationship than I ever dreamed possible.

Lee and Jerry

We started out writing this book to assist fathers and sons in recognizing their own yearnings and wounds. But we soon discovered as many women were interested in this material as were men. After a number of discussions with the women in our lives, we soon realized the reason for this. We men carry the conflicts we have with our fathers into our relationships with our wives and lovers. And as we come to terms with our father–son relationships, women can share the benefits with us through the deeper intimacy we can enjoy with them.

We are also reminded that women are affected by father–son relationships in as many ways as we men are. First, they have fathers, and those fathers were sons themselves, whose relationships may have been rocky. Second, a woman's husband or lover may very well have a difficult relationship with his father, creating tension which she can feel quite acutely.

The bottom line in all of this is that we quickly came to realize that this book was not just for and about men. It was also a book for women. If it helped men better understand their father–son relationships, it could also help women feel closer to the men in their lives—their husbands, fathers, and sons.

While this book uncovers the unseen sources of conflict in father–son relationships, the good news is that *healing is possible*. We share our own stories and efforts in healing by being as completely honest as we can. The reader will find places in this book where anger, guilt, and fear are voiced and places where forgiveness and healing occur. No two readers come from the same place. There may be times when the writing on forgiveness frustrates you because you're still angry, or times when the writing on anger frustrates you because you're ready for forgiveness. Read the book as a whole and try to honor all your feelings. The greatest source of healing is not the information in the book, but your feelings and reactions as you read the information.

The process of writing this book came about because we are both passionately committed in continuing our efforts to be at peace with ourselves. We know that healing our relationship is essential to this peace. While we both find much support in the spiritual principles in *A Course in Miracles,* we believe there are many different and effective pathways, ranging from therapy and counseling to many religious and spiritual paths.

As long as there are unresolved feelings and issues (anger, fear, guilt, shame) with our fathers, our relationships with women will be negatively affected. In our own lives and those with whom we have worked, the repressed issues with our fathers will get played out in our relationships with women. For years I (Lee) had a difficult time with anger. I would occasionally feel rage deep in my gut and explode in anger directed towards my wife. Not until seeing that much of my rage was anger that I carried for my father—anger that he never expressed towards my mother—could I actually begin to do something about it.

The dynamics of how sons and fathers relate to each other undoubtedly plays a major role in how men relate to women. As women begin to understand more about why fathers and sons behave in the way they do, they will be able to see the fear that men have of their own emotions and vulnerability. It is this fear that often causes communication between men and women to break down.

Men's deep inner fears, stemming from the relationships with their fathers, can literally cause them to become anesthetized—numbed from being aware of their emotions. They can then be perceived by the women in their lives as callous or insensitive. It is the opposite that is really true. Men actually have an abundance of feelings, but are so afraid that they wouldn't touch them with a ten-foot pole. Perhaps that is another reason that so many men become workaholics; men too busy "doing" have no time to feel.

Fathers and sons can find many ways of either hiding or denying their fears. We found that "professionalism" can be used as a defense against fear and coming to grips with one's own emotions and feelings. Perhaps one of the most unique aspects of this book is that it is written by a father and a son who both have professional careers in psychiatry and psychology. Professional training and skills in helping others do not give us immunity from the open wounds of our painful past. We both have had, at different times in our lives, our fair share of personal therapy. Yet it is apparent that much unfinished business between us remains buried in our minds.

We found our professional training can actually hinder healing. It is tempting to hide behind intellectualizations, rationalizations, and psychological language. At times, our so-called psychological "know-how" became another layer of defense covering our love and creating a loss of intimacy. This is not to say that our personal therapy has not been valuable. In fact, without our own psychotherapy this book may have never come about. Many people, men or women, who read this book and want to continue with their healing may find entering counseling or psychotherapy will further the process.

Sharing pain, grief, and vulnerability can bring about forgiving our grandfathers, fathers, sons, and ourselves. Then we can experience honesty, compassion, gentleness, kindness, tenderness, and self-acceptance. Opening ourselves to our inner pains and anger, and listening to the frightened child within each of us, is the way toward healing.

To promote any healing, willingness is needed. We must be willing to remove the blocks to our inner world, so that we may recognize and experience who we are now and who we can become. It is our choice whether we continue to hold on to pain and play the game of guilt and blame or decide to let it go and live in the present.

In the hearts of many fathers and sons lives a lost, frightened little boy, uncertain in which direction to go, and longing for an authentic relationship with his father. Likewise, many women are finding that the same lost sons are reaching out to them, often with less than happy results. In our work, we have seen lost fathers and lost sons reaching out to each other to find the closeness and intimacy they have missed for much of their lives. So many men are finding that they have suffered much pain and fear of love. Fathers discover that many of the problems they have with their sons are similar to the problems they had with their own fathers. Fathers and sons are finding that forgiveness is the great healer and the key to their happiness. It is forgiveness that allows fathers and sons to find themselves and to be lost no more. And it is forgiveness that can bring men into more complete relationships with the women in their lives.

The healing we began as we shared our inner, secret dialogues—first with ourselves, and now with each other—is at the heart of this book. By making a sincere and determined effort to truly take responsibility for our own anger and guilt, and by sharing our vulnerability and pain, we were able to see each other differently. It allowed us to experience a deep healing and reach new unlimited dimensions of love.

As fathers and sons read this book—together or individually—hopefully they may find the strength to listen to each other non-defensively, to tell their truths, and to share their vulnerability. And as women read this book, they may gain a deeper understanding for, and connection with, their spouses, fathers, and sons. Through this process we can all collectively begin a healing that was perhaps once thought impossible.

It is through this work, that we have each found a greater ability to forgive, more patience to accept, and the compassion to love more deeply. It is through this work that we have rediscovered each other.

In order not to interrupt the flow of the book's intimate dialogue, we have added an appendix which contains lists and exercises. Also, information in the stories of people we have worked with has been changed in order to ensure confidentiality. Any resemblance you may find between these stories and someone you know is purely coincidental.

A Note to the Reader

You will find this book different than most you have read. Because of this we wanted to make a few comments about why it is different and how you might approach it.

The main feeling of our work is contained in the very personal letters we wrote back and forth to each other over a period of many months. We share these with the hope that readers who may be seeking a deeper understanding of their own father–son relationships can see that they are not alone.

Our letters reveal, perhaps best of all, the story of conflict, inner struggle, doubt, fear, and love that can lead us all to either peaceful resolutions or deeper wisdom about our father–son relationships. If you wish, first read only the letters themselves, allowing the story we tell to unfold much as it would if you were reading a novel or autobiography. It's easy to pick out these letters from the rest of the text: they are printed in a different style of type.

At the end of each chapter you'll find reflections and guidelines which we (Lee and Jerry) found helpful in the months we were writing to each other. We felt it would be helpful to our readers to include this more reflective material. You'll find insights here that grew out of our work together. They can be supportive resources for you and your loved ones as you look at these issues in your own life. Just as they did for us, these insights can become stepping stones for you, marking the path to better, happier relationships.

Whether you read for the adventure of mutual discovery contained in the letters, or to seek new insights about the fathers and sons in your life, we hope this book will make at least a small contribution toward mending the ties that bind.

PART ONE

The Search

When I look back, there is a blind spot in the car.
It is some bit of my father I keep not seeing.
I cannot remember years of my childhood.
Some parts of me I cannot find now.

I intended that; I threw some parts of me away
at ten; others at twenty; a lot around twenty-eight.
I wanted to thin myself out as a wire is thinned.
Is there enough left of me now to be honest?

ROBERT BLY, "NIGHT FROGS"

ONE

Listening
to the Yearning

If we are not careful,
life can be a game of hide and seek.
We hide the love within us from ourselves.
We then seek it outside ourselves,
where it can never be found.

Today a son makes his mark in the world of work by his own deeds. Independence, achievement, and competitiveness are all honored traits for young men in our culture. None of these coincides with reuniting with one's father. Indeed it is just the opposite. The role of the young man is to replace the old, "to put them out to pasture." These traits also encourage an avoidance of a man's inner life, where his feelings of loss, sadness, and need for his father reside.

JERROLD LEE SHAPIRO, *THE MEASURE OF MAN*

Dear Dad,

It's important to write you in my own hand. I want to be close to you and for you to hear me more deeply than you usually do. Computers, word processors, and faxes create speed at the cost of intimacy. I want you to feel the paper which my hand crosses as I write to you. Maybe this will bring us closer.

Recently my friend Joe sent me some books on fatherhood. As I read them, my head is swimming with images and many new and unexplored feelings have arisen. This is surprising to me because I thought I had dealt with so many of my issues. I am not as angry with you as I once was. I have worked hard on being an adult child of an alcoholic, especially my low self-esteem and co-dependence. I have come not to be so intensely concerned with pleasing you and most of the time I am able to feel my own independence.

All my psychotherapy, training, and talks with you are in the background of my consciousness. In this present moment, I find myself face to face with you. I'm both scared and excited. The process we have begun will free something vital in me and change my life forever. I know that my freedom is not going to be handed to me. I know that you would like to offer me my freedom and unleash my potential and wholeness, without my having to struggle for it. My growth will not come without some struggle. I also know that I can no longer grow without you.

I have always known that you love me, yet somehow I have never been able to fully let you in. I stay on the defensive, somehow thinking that the past will repeat itself. I talk to you about my job, kids, and the weather—but I don't let you into my real inner life: my concerns, my dreams, my pain. Tears well up in me as I write. I have no idea what to do with

5

these feelings of hope, fear, sadness, and longing. They are too powerful to enter into and too powerful to turn away from. I'm not paralyzed by these emotions. Just sitting and feeling, sitting and writing, is enough right now.

I have hidden inside myself, behind high walls of self-righteousness and judgment. I have moved to different cities, states, and even countries. I ran by telling myself that I didn't need you. In some odd way everything that I did was in some way running from you. Having a good and successful life was a statement of independence, and my need for independence was in part running from your dominating personality. I have run from both of us for a long time. I am not sure how to return, or even if returning is the answer. Perhaps we will find new territory where our love can unfold in each of us.

I also feel that your father is present in all of this. In the past I have been so focused on what you did or didn't give me, that I forgot that you too had a father. I want to know more about your relationship with Grandpa. I too am a father now and am in awe of the magnitude of all that fatherhood is. It is important for me to stand in awe.

For too long I have seen your role as my father as one-dimensional: What can or cannot I get from you? Being a father, I now know the joys and the turmoil; the pull of wanting to be home with my kids while I drive to the office to be close to others, discussing our innermost truths in psychotherapy. At times, I have to gather together the last remaining parts of me to be present at home at the end of the day.

Sometimes I fail and am a little more than argumentative and distant. I love being a father more than I have ever loved anything before. This love for my own process and for my daughters, Jalena and Lexi, has opened my ability to love you as well. I have kept you distant from me, but never admitted it to either of us. I want to bring you back into my life.

As Robert Bly, Sam Keen, and John Lee have written before me—I hunger for my father. At this stage it has more to do with me allowing you in than anything else.

Dad, there have been times when I felt that I was made of, or a product of, something defective. There have been times when I have felt that I am the product of something so good that I can never reach or match it. Both feelings left me impotent and weak. Robert Bly has written on how many men have fought their fathers, the dark father, to overcome them. He also writes of men who have tried to rise above their fathers, flying high, transcending, leaving them below. I have tried both and have failed at both.

In our relationship, I have attempted healing by working on and attacking your shadow or dark side. As I have walked through my life I have been blind to so many of the shadowy images within my own consciousness. I have chosen to focus on your darkness instead of fully examining my own. Lately, I have allowed myself a measure of acceptance, and I have allowed myself to see my shadow. We cannot join as long as your shadow is the only darkness that I see.

Developing empathy, compassion, kindness, tolerance, and understanding for you is a prerequisite for our journey. Embracing our individual and collective shadows is an integral part of this development. There is a quote from *A Course in Miracles* that has been helpful to me in this:

> The escape from darkness involves two stages: First, the recognition that darkness cannot hide. This step usually entails fear. Second, the recognition that there is nothing you want to hide even if you could. This step brings escape from fear. When you have become willing to hide nothing, you will not only be willing to enter communion but will understand peace and joy. (*A Course in Miracles*, second edition, Text, page 11)

In the past it has been painful for me to have a strong father like you. I remember with some shame and embarrassment the time as a teenager that I physically fought you in our garage. I had been internally raging at you for years and was sick of feeling controlled and overlooked. I wanted to go someplace and you told me that I couldn't go. I thought that maybe physically I could conquer you. My shame weakened me more than my rage strengthened me. I gave up and lost. And so it was with tennis and many other areas, trying to conquer you, only to give up.

To no avail, I kept trying to fly above you and ascend into the heavens. Somebody's chance comment, "you're following in your father's footsteps," would violently throw me from the sky to the hard ground below. I could not beat you or fly above you. Today there is no happier statement. Now perhaps I can meet you, join with you, love you, and most importantly, allow you to love me.

Together

My sword has not been sharp enough to slay you,
letting me be the victor only in my dreams.
My wings have not been strong enough
to fly the sky above you.
Perhaps this has been God's hand in my life,
guiding me on the path,
to teach me where not to go,
so that I may arrive where love is.
I pray now that my heart will open to yours,
and we may meet in the fields where fathers and sons
lay on their backs, head to head,
and look up to the heavens together.

Dad, I have hidden from and fought you; I have left you, pushed you, and tried to rise above you; I have idolized and demonized you; I have blamed, loved, and hated you; I have judged you, run *from* you, and run *to* you; I have played and competed with you; I have lied and raged at you; I have needed you and denied you. Now all I want is to let you into my life more fully and completely. I'm grateful you are in my life and I love you very much.

Love,
Lee

Dear Lee,

Your letter touched the very center of my soul. I felt frustrated because I immediately wanted to hug you and thank you for your love, for your tenderness, and for your sensitivity. Your honesty and desire to be closer opens the door to further dialogue. My heart became more open, tender, and vulnerable because of your letter.

We can both remember times when we never thought our relationship could ever be healed. In looking back, it seems as if I had my demons to conquer and you had yours. As you come out of your dark closet to share the things that need to be said, I can only be encouraged to share with you my innermost thoughts and feelings.

You mentioned times when I was your enemy. I am sure that unconsciously, in a strange way, you also became my enemy. When you became addicted to drugs, I told myself, "He is addicted to drugs because of me." At the time I was not able to see any of the effects of my love or any of the positive things that I had done as your father. In seeing only the darkness, I told myself that if I hadn't been an alcoholic this never would have never happened. I told myself over and over again, "Jerry, this is all your fault."

No matter what I did, I didn't seem able to help you. Your own addiction repeated my painful past. I fell into an unresolved misery. You reminded me of my guilt and I concluded that I must have done a lousy job of fathering.

In the days of your childhood I didn't consider myself an alcoholic. I thought of myself as a heavy drinker who could easily tolerate large amounts of alcohol. I was deep into denial and used alcohol to bury my pain. I took false strength in the fact that I never drank in the daytime. It must have affected you gravely to see me as one person in the daytime, and a different person at night. I used alcohol to rid myself of depression as well as the pain I had from chronic degenerative disc problems. It wasn't until 1975 when I consciously began on a spiritual pathway that I chose to stop drinking. Your own addiction problems caused me much agony because I still felt I was the cause of all your ailments.

The doctors assured me that your back problems were organic and diagnosed it as Scheuermann's disease. I remember that you had over a dozen hospitalizations. There were times that I wondered if your back problems—which painfully mirrored my own—were going to keep you down throughout your whole life. I felt overwhelming guilt and thought I deserved all the rejection that came from you. It proved to me what I was already thinking, that I was unlovable and not deserving of your love.

You have asked me about my early feelings ... what was going on inside me at the time of your infancy. Those where the most tender of all the years, where the hugging and cuddling seemed continuous. I wanted to stop time and somehow capture the experience so that I could always have it and re-experience it whenever I wished. Every part of me wanted to honor the faith and trust you had in me then. During those days, hugs lasted a long time. Today our hugs are too brief. I miss those long hugs when you were a small child, when it was not unmanly to hug in a timeless way.

When I watch you with your daughters, many of my early memories come back and I smile. I see what a very special loving relationship you have with your children. I hope that you might be able to identify with me and know how very special it was to have you and Greg as my children.

I have many good memories of the vacations we had. Your mom and I and you and Greg traveled to Arizona to visit my parents, rode horses, and went hiking. I remember the cowboy hats that you loved so much and the fishing trips to the Sierras, San Francisco Bay, and Lake Lagunitas. I am sure that during those times, our family looked like a most loving, happy, healthy, family. I rarely missed a back-to-school night or a little league baseball game. I remember countless hours playing basketball and pool with you and your brother.

There were the hot dog and marshmallow roasts in Carmel and the wonderful times we shared with each other at the beach. I remember piles of presents at Christmas. There was a fleeting thought that I felt at the time that perhaps your mother and I were over-gratifying you and Greg. Or to put it in simpler terms, we were spoiling both of you because of our own unmet needs.

You asked me to tell you about my relationship with my dad. He didn't talk much about his feelings. In fact, we talked very little. I knew he loved me, but I did want him to be different. The unfinished business I had with my dad that I was not consciously aware of at the time, had to affect how I treated you and your brother.

You asked how I felt, what was going on inside of me in those days, when you were a young boy. I was so out of touch with my feelings that I was numb inside. I was not able to communicate my own feelings to myself, let alone to those who were close to me. I was self-absorbed in my workaholism. Like my father I worked long hours. I made hospital rounds at 6:30 AM and rarely got home before 7:30 PM. There were also many evening meetings I had to attend, making me unavailable to you or anyone else in the family. I did not recognize that I was using my work to protect me from the pain of looking inside.

Although I remember many loving things that happened between us during your childhood, it is hard to believe that there was enough wholesome, valid communication since I was so often under the influence of Scotch and wine in the evenings. I remember your mom trying to get me to spend more time at home. It infuriated me when she would compare me negatively with other fathers in the neighborhood. It just increased the guilt I was trying to deny. I remember with deep embarrassment telling her that my patients came first . . . and then my family. When she heard this, she erupted with anger, causing even more emotional distance between us.

I felt guilty that you and Greg were exposed to so many arguments and slammed doors and tension between your mom and me. You grew up not knowing what unpredictable events were around the corner. We were a family that looked good on the outside but had too many problems on the inside. I desperately wish to go back and relive that time, spending real quality time with you. I would present you with a model to follow of a father who is strong yet vulnerable, rather than weak, undependable, and unavailable.

I had a lot of friends, but none in whom I would dare confide. My painful shyness was very successfully covered up. I never saw myself as much of a risk taker, and yet I was very vocal about my anti-Vietnam war feelings in spite of the fact that I was attacked and accused of being a Communist by my medical society.

My feelings of inadequacy were in all directions: fatherhood, husbandhood, just being a person. I wrote many professional papers but I never felt any of them were great. During those days I was very competitive with my two brothers and never felt that I could equal them. I saw myself as dumb and clumsy and wished I could be as brilliant and smart as they were. I saw them as extremely successful in their careers and seriously doubted that I could ever be successful in my chosen career. My childhood feelings of inadequacy shadowed me through adulthood. I always felt I was on the outside of things and that if people really and truly knew what I was like they would reject me. They would only like the costume I was wearing, not the real me.

I felt guilty that you were not given either a formal or an informal religious or spiritual education. I was surprised and more than pleased when you began to show an interest in following a spiritual path. *A Course in Miracles* had become my heartbeat and spiritual pathway, bringing me more inner peace than I ever thought possible. It was my hope and desire that you might also find the inner peace of God within you.

Lee, I know there is still more anger and disappointment at the unmet expectations you had of me as your father. It's important that the anger and disappointment come out, no matter how much either of us might be afraid. My hope and intention is to remain defenseless as we work together to heal our relationship.

Coming together like this is a most unique opportunity for both of us to heal. I feel very blessed and fortunate to be doing this with you. That we have both come so far and are still willing to reach out to each other is beyond my furthest hope. Lee, I love you. I could not be more proud of you. You walk your talk and have become not just a son, but a friend and a teacher.

It is clear to me that although we have done much in the areas of forgiveness, there is still much more work to be done. I especially realize that the quality of our relationship has to do with my continued forgiveness of my father for not being quite the man I wanted him to be.

Thanks for being there. And thanks for your courage for opening the door and keeping it open. More than thanks for your willingness to transform our relationship into one of friendship.

Love,
Dad

Dear Dad,
Recently I have paid more attention to my thoughts and feelings about our relationship, both current and in the past. I have allowed myself time without demanding that I understand or figure anything out. I would like to share some of my process with you.

At this point in my life, it feels very liberating not to hold back in discussing events and emotions that come up with you. I had to get over being afraid of hurting you in order for us to become closer.

You speak of the father that you wanted to be. I would like to hear more about this. My guess is that you and I, and most fathers, want similar things in fulfilling our roles as fathers. What got in your way? That question makes my gut tense and I feel myself regress about thirty years. I am afraid. There is a lump in my throat and tears mass to fall. The frightened little boy in me asks, "Is it me? What's wrong with me? Am I the reason you are not the father you wanted to be? Am I the cause of constant tension between you and Mom?"

I don't want my children to ask these questions. Although I feel that I am a very good father, I am still not completely the father I would like to be. Though I am patient I still occasionally lose my composure; though I allow my kids free expression I am still probably overly concerned and protective. It would help me to hear more from you. Healing our relationship, present and past, is the greatest gift that you can give me and your grandchildren. I wish more fathers and sons would realize this.

I am more open with you and sharing about my life, but it is not easy for me. I still fear your judgment and want to please you. Getting beyond these feelings to my authenticity is no easy task. The more I do it, the more natural it becomes. What can be more natural and beautiful than a son turning to his father for support, guidance, and friendship?

Sometimes after I talk with you, I vacillate between being angry that you misunderstood what I said and being ashamed and afraid that you did understand. This translates into my need for you to know me, and not just what I do, but who I am. At the same time I am afraid that you won't like what you see.

Sometimes I feel that you take one or two things that I say and then fill in the blanks with your own perceptions and ideas, somehow missing me. Other times I feel that I am able to say one or two things and you see all of me. Frankly, both have pissed me off in the past. I now realize what a split mind I have had. Part of me wanted healing and closeness with you, while I held onto my anger and pushed you away. I am trying to trust the process of sharing in the most genuine way that I can, and be who I am in the moment. Whatever comes up, comes up. We can either deal with it or not. But if we can't, I still feel closer to both you and myself. I don't want to hide from you or anybody else. Mostly, I don't want to hide from myself.

In 1977 I dropped out of graduate school in my second semester because I had to give a three-to-five-minute oral presentation in front of ten people. I was so afraid of being seen, I felt that I just couldn't hide being screwed up any longer. I moved into an isolated house in the country and saw very few people. All I did was stay home, take drugs, and drink. It seemed impossible just go to the store.

As I write this I am both saddened and grateful. I have worked through so much. Now, after a lot of internal work, I am showing up in life. I am still amazed when I walk on a stage and lecture in front of hundreds of people. I am even more amazed when I let them see who I am. I don't want you to feel guilty. That is not my purpose in sharing with you. I just want you to know what it was like for me.

About five years ago you and I spent three days together at Big Sur and began to directly talk about our relationship. I had invited you down and at the time I was not sure exactly what I had in mind. I did know that I wanted to try to begin to get closer. You have referred to this trip as being very positive and I agree, but it was just a beginning.

You immediately wanted to go public with what we were doing. Even though I still denied many of my feelings, I agreed to do a workshop in Santa Rosa with you for fathers and sons, entitled "Healing Father–Son Relationships." We helped a lot of men, but this experience perpetuated a wound for me. I always felt that I had to look good in front of an audience. At our recent father–son workshop in Seattle, I broke out of this at the end of the first day. I did not know what I was doing. In the middle of the workshop I felt that you were treating me the same as when I was a kid: controlling, intimidating, and running the show. Rather than sit on it, I confronted you with my feelings during the workshop and we worked it out in front of everybody. I think that this was not only powerful for me, but also helped those attending the workshop.

It is only this week that I realized I was saying to you,

"Dad, I love you, but I can't always be thinking about looking good in front of an audience. It is important for me to be there with you, but not always thinking about how the audience sees us." I now know that you have no need for me to make you look good. I am not sure that you ever did. But somehow all this affected me.

You say that you have been tempted to claim responsibility for my behaviors that resemble your behaviors—your alcoholism and other negative personality traits. You also have some wonderful personality traits and I have no doubt that who I am has been positively influenced by who you are.

There is a big difference between influence and cause. Cause implies that we have no choice in changing or growing beyond. Then I would be stuck with all the bad stuff forever. Influence implies that we affect each other, but still have choices, as adults, to work through, grow, and change. I was influenced positively and negatively by you. Though I wish you had been around more and that alcohol had not been so prevalent in our family, I would not change the many ways you have demonstrated sensitivity and growth. As I bring up the old wounds so they can be healed, I would like to share with you your positive influence. *Before I could see any of the positive lessons you taught me, I had to work through the anger and blame I had.*

You taught me that nothing is impossible. I have been blessed by learning this. I am now and have always been amazed at the things you do, the people you meet, and the situations that you create. We have both had to learn how to be assertive without being intimidating and overly aggressive. Nonetheless I rarely see impossible situations, and am always looking for creative solutions and opportunities.

You taught me about service. Though you may have been a workaholic, beneath this there was something very genuine.

You wanted to serve your fellow human beings. I was never prouder than when my friends would come to you for advice, or they would ask me to ask you. There was some irony in this because of my difficulty in sharing with you, but it did build in me the value of integrity and service.

You taught me about racial equality and choice of lifestyles. Prejudice was so foreign to me I couldn't understand how anybody could think that way. You taught me that every human being deserves equal rights and opportunity. But you didn't only do it with words. You reached out and worked with minorities and the learning disabled. You saw and did something about the wrongs of the Vietnam War. You taught me that having an opinion that differed from others was all right.

You taught me that taking risks is all right. The other day I was down at the beach in Carmel and climbed some of the rocks I climbed as a kid. At first I thought you had been crazy and I would never let my kids climb these rocks. Dad, because you allowed me to take risks as a kid, I am not afraid of much out there in the world. I am not afraid to be alone for days in the wilderness. I am not afraid to be alone in the middle of a strange country. I am not afraid to push my physical limits.

You taught me that competition is not how we derive our self-worth. I never felt that I had to beat somebody else in order to be all right with myself. I have felt competition with you in the past, but somehow the more positive lesson stuck with me.

You taught me that having nice things was fine, but I never learned from you that they mattered much. I have never felt that money and material possessions were overly important.

You taught me self-direction and self-reliance, that I must find the purpose and meaning in my life. You taught me something called choice and freedom.

You taught me about gentleness, sensitivity, and being a

man. Displays of machismo are unnecessary. As a teenager I remember some of the negative aspects of masculinity my friends' fathers laid on them and was grateful that you never did. You taught me that there was strength in gentleness.

You taught me that change is possible. When I was 18 years old, you began to really change your life. You began a spiritual path and became much more focused on the present moment. You stopped drinking and became more involved in service, founding the first Center for Attitudinal Healing. For many years I didn't believe in those changes. I saw you more as a hypocrite than a changed man. I was wrong. You really began to grow. Since I have been an adult, your life has demonstrated to me that we always have a choice. Through your growth, you have also taught me the value of a spiritual life.

I am sure that there is an another side to everything I've written here. For example, though I learned gentleness from you, I did not learn what to do with my rage. But my purpose here is to remind you that it is okay to take responsibility for your role in being my father. Just be sure that you do it completely, including the positive. You taught me a lot of wonderful things about life. This is because you are a wonderful man.

Peace be to you, Dad. Thank you for what you have given me—not just the good stuff, but also the opportunity to grow through the pain as well. In writing this letter it has also helped me with my own parenting. I don't have to be perfect, just available. Some of my mistakes in parenting may provide my daughters with their greatest growth later in life. I need to trust the process of parenting, and see it as life-long, rather than having to get it right every moment.

Love,
Lee

Dear Lee,
I read your last letter several times. Your remarks about the things you learned from me were most tender and loving. Any father would feel proud to receive such words from his son.

I acknowledge that I do give you double messages. I have been guilty of telling you I want a closer relationship with you and encouraged you to share your inner feelings with me, then didn't listen with unconditional love and became defensive, interruptive, and stopped listening. I want to do a better job at listening without defensiveness. I really do want to know how you feel inside and have an intimate relationship with you. I want it to be safe and desirable for you not to have any withholds from me. On the other hand, your statements, unfortunately, sometimes get interpreted by my twisted ego into—"I am to blame for your unhappiness." I don't believe that is your intention.

At times there's a part of me that says, "I wish he had not said that. It is not my perception. I wish he would not bring things up that make me look at his and my own shared pain." Sometimes it seems as if it is too much for me to face. I think it's the same part of me that also says, "Avoid all pain at any cost." Unfortunately, the cost has been the quality of my relationship with you.

I apologize for all those double messages and will do my best to be more consistent in not letting my ego get in the way. I recently saw on a t-shirt, "I Don't Have an Attitude Problem. You Have a Perception Problem." Sometimes this is the message you and I give to each other. We both know that no one is perfect. Yet there are times that we have put that expectation on each other, or ourselves, only to be sadly and painfully disappointed.

Lee, I remember when you were about three years old, you hurt your finger and came running to me full of tears. I kissed your finger and held you until all the pain went away. There have been so many times in your life, as a child and an adult, that I wished you still believed that I could heal all things for you—like magic!

I was most pleased to see the videotape of your recent lecture, "Healing the Addictive Mind" at Lake Arrowhead. I had copies made of the audio portion and sent them to many of my friends with such a feeling of pride. Last month I thought I was sending a tape of the musical version of my and Diane's book, *Me First and the Gimme Gimmes* to our friends in Maryland. I accidentally sent your tape instead. The miracle of this accident was that they liked it so much they insisted on talking to you about giving a lecture. God* certainly operates in wonderful ways, and the angels must have a sense of humor.

I am so pleased for you, for your personal successes, and your devotion and sensitivity to helping so many others. You continue to teach me about compassion, love, forgiveness, patience, and perseverance.

I think it takes a lot of courage to work with your dad and get past the old competitive drives that used to be there. Your willingness to go through your pain helps me get past my reluctance to go through mine. I can't thank you enough for this.

Love,
Dad

---

*When we speak of "God," as we do throughout the book, we understand it as *a power greater than ourselves*. We recognize, of course, that there are many people who call this power by different names.

Beginning the Process of Healing

For men and women, it's not necessarily important to figure out what you are going to do at this point. It's important to pay attention to your own perceptions, thoughts, and feelings. If any one letter or section particularly moves you, spend a little extra time with that material. To get the most out of this information, pay attention to your thoughts, feelings, memories, fears, and hopes as you read.

In order to heal, the first step is to recognize that sharing one's vulnerability and tenderness is not a sign of weakness, but a strength. This is especially true for men. We need to unlearn some of the misconceptions we were taught by our old role models. Secondly, every relationship can be healed because our thoughts and perceptions are all that are needed to change. And last, death, geography, temperament of others, the past, guilt, and anger are only obstacles to be overcome in the journey towards healing. As you will see later, even if you never knew your father or son or they are deceased, or emotionally unavailable, there are still feelings within yourself that can to be explored and healed.

When I (Lee) wrote my dad the first letter in this book, I had no idea if I would have the courage to give it to him. I was totally frightened of what would happen. Looking back, I was as afraid of healing as I was of rejection. There was no response my father could have given that would not have had been received without some element of fear.

There were two rules that we both agreed on. The first was to do our best not to do anything if healing was not the goal. If anger were expressed, it was for the purpose of working through the anger. This was in contrast to how we had often used anger in the past, which was to make the other person feel guilty. The second rule was to do our best to talk about our own experiences rather than blaming the other person. Having a goal of healing and letting go of blame, healing began to slowly take place.

You may find it helpful to begin as we did and write a letter to your father or son. Tell them how you felt growing up and how you feel now. Talk about fears and hopes, loss and forgotten dreams. Don't worry about covering everything in this letter, the purpose is to open the door within *you* to healing. The emphasis is on your healing, *not* the other person having to change. You may never even have anybody else read this letter.

Another helpful task that each of us did was to talk to other men about what our experience of our father was and is now. It is amazing that men usually do not know much about each other's fathers. Once we start talking, we not only begin healing, but we also get to know our male friends in a deeper way.

We have shared these letters with hundreds of men and women that have attended our workshops on father-son relationships. The most common comment is "How do you get so open and vulnerable? I could never do that with my father/son." The single most important change we made in our relationship is very simple: We *decided* that we were tired of how it was and wanted something different. We made the conscious decision that no matter what occurred we were going to be open and keep going.

There were many times when one or both of us shut off from the other, from being too hurt or angry. We kept going. There were many times that we thought to ourselves "I have better things to do with my time than to deal with stuff that happened thirty or sixty years ago. There is nothing that I could do about that now." We kept going.

The emphasis began with both of us wanting to have a guarantee of acceptance from the other person. We found that this was not always the case. Sometimes when we thought we were saying something well intended, the other would become hurt or defensive. We found that the emphasis of acceptance had to be on self-acceptance. There are no guarantees about how the other person is going to react, but there is a guarantee that if we bring up our old shame, guilt, and anger, and work towards letting it go, we will have a greater degree of self-acceptance. Self-acceptance is akin to forgiveness, and forgiveness is the key to inner peace.

We have found that in the process of attempting to heal our own relationship with each other, the following stepping stones have been most helpful.

- Have a willingness to open up to the possibility of enjoying a more intimate, deep, and honest relationship with each other.

- Be willing to share our own vulnerability.

- Tell our own story and truly listen to one another without judgment.

- Take on the responsibility of facing and experiencing our own anger without dumping it onto the other person.

- Recognize that it is only our own thoughts that hurt us.

- Believe that there are only two emotions, love or fear, and that the other person is either giving love or is fearful, giving a call of help for love.

- Become aware that no one is to blame and have a willingness to let go of guilt.

- Recognize that only we, ourselves, have the power to decide if we are worthy of love.

- Recognize that peace of mind comes to us when we are defenseless.

- Giving everything to our Higher Power and choosing to let God come first in our relationships.

- Awaken to the truth that Love is the essence of our being and everyone else's being, our true and only reality, that love is all there is and everything that there is, and that love and forgiveness are always the answer to any conflict that we may face with each other.

TWO

The
Fantasized Father

*Healing is learning to have the courage
to experience the pain of our unexpressed grief.*

Once we stop waiting for the father we can never have, we will start healing our deepest wound and start being our real selves.

JOHN LEE, "AT MY FATHER'S WEDDING"

Dear Dad,

As a boy I had a few favorite places in the hills above our house in Tiburon. I loved those hills and felt most at home when I was surrounded by them. In one spot the grass grew so tall that I could lie down and disappear, swallowed in the moist smell of the dirt and tickled by green and golden stalks of grass brushing my face.

There was comfort in being alone. I found peace through disappearing into the hills with only the blue sky dotted with clouds in my vision. I am not sure why I wanted to disappear, but I am grateful for those hills. My guess is that I needed safety, grounding, and holding. The hills did this for me. They became my father in this way.

At some level I wanted your arms to be the grass and the moistness of your fatherly smell to be the hills. I wanted your eyes to be the sky that I gazed into. You were not there all the time. My adult-self knows that you couldn't have possibly been there each time I needed you, but I fantasized that you could. The hills became my way of making this true.

Lying on my back on my hill, I used to play games with the clouds. I would try to make them into different shapes. I was usually successful. The wind would wash the wisps of white into shapes that my mind would author. Like the clouds, I tried to make you into things that you were not. Long after I stopped playing "cloud shaping," I still tried to change you into a different man.

At about age five, as I lay in my room, I distinctly remember having this conversation with myself, "If I fell out of my window, Dad would be there to catch me. But he couldn't do that because he is all the way at the end of the hall asleep with Mom. But he would be able to do it because he is magic."

I went to sleep that night believing in magic. How many times I must have been disappointed. As I write this now, I feel the child in me beginning to cry. I wish the magic never disappeared. I wish you never became mortal, with all the disappointments that come with having a mortal for a father.

I hated how you always claimed to be "unmechanical." I don't think it was the fact that you were that bothered me. It was how you always seemed to use it as an excuse. I wanted you to be competent and involved, and I always thought this was an excuse not to be. For a while I thought I had to be "unmechanical" too. Now when I fix things around our house, or make things, I think of you. I believe that you had fears about being completely involved with life, and probably, as I do, had fears of failing.

I used to wish that you would be more athletic and competent. I remember you racing our little Sunfish sailboat. I would watch you struggle in last place and want you to either quit or do something to win. I don't think it is an accident that both of your sons are very athletic and mechanical. Nor do I think it is an accident that Greg has become a world-class sailor and I have become a commercial pilot. It seems that we both (in these examples and many more) may have unconsciously tried to become our fantasies of you. I don't think this is uncommon for sons.

You always had a big problem with directions. This used to bother me. My fantasy was for you to be a man that was confident in his ability to get from point A to point B, or at least to remember which way to turn when you came out of the restroom. I laugh about this now because this quality is actually something that endears you to me. It is part of who you are, and I love this trait in you.

I wanted you to be more present with me and more interested in me. I wanted you to be competent at everything you did and do everything. I wanted you to always take care of Mom. I wanted you to stand up to Mom. I wanted you to make everything in the family all right. Though I don't feel like blaming you now, these unreal expectations have profoundly affected me. Specifically:

I wanted your full love and support, and yet for years I could not say "I love you."

I wanted to be as competent and successful a psychologist as you were a psychiatrist. Yet for years I cringed in a combination of anger and shame when anybody said I was following in your footsteps.

I was angry at you for divorcing Mom, even though it was probably the right thing to do. I vowed that when I married I would never divorce. My first marriage lasted only six months.

For most of my life I wanted you to be available to me, but when you finally were, I found myself unavailable to you—full of anger and doubt.

I fantasized about an all-accepting, non-critical father. My wife's most common response to me during a conflict between us is that I am intimidating and critical.

I wanted guidance and support from you. Because I didn't receive much of either, I never learned how to accept help. I felt that I should do it myself. As an adult, when people have offered me help I have been defensive and ashamed.

I wanted you to relax and just be with me. Sometimes you did but for the most part, you demonstrated that something was wrong if you did not or could not work a minimum of 12 hours a day.

I have chosen not to work long hours and I enjoy spending half of each day with my kids. But, like you, I have not missed a day of work for illness in years. That is not to say that I have not been sick. It just seems next to impossible for me to take time for myself when I need it.

I wanted you to be strong around Mom. You worked hard, had no personal life to speak of, and drank and became depressed rather than angry. In the past I have tended to need to make sure that women are always happy, and I married a woman who has a difficult time with anger.

It saddens me when I look back and see all the ways that I pushed away your good qualities while wanting you to become what you were not. No wonder I was so confused and unhappy. The most psychologically interesting dynamic to me is how I chose a career that follows in your footsteps, yet wanted to completely deny this.

My healing of the father-wound has taken me in two directions that seem opposite, but I have found must go together. My career choice is a good example. Before, when people said I was following in your footsteps, the reason I felt anger and shame was that unconsciously I had to separate myself from you. Everything in me said, "Be different from Dad." I needed my own separate identity.

When someone suggested I was not separating myself from you, but instead identifying with you, this triggered all my alarms. I felt ashamed that I was not an individual in my own right; I was just like you, and at that time I didn't like you very much.

To identify with our fathers means that we embrace how we are like them and attempt to understand our lives in that context. To separate from them means to be and become very different from them. The key to my healing has been in recognizing that both processes are imperative: Every man must simultaneously identify with his father and separate himself from him. In this culture we tend to deny the former (identifying) and accentuate the latter (separation). Until we are willing to consciously identify how much we are like our fathers, our attempts at separation actually make us more unconsciously like them.

The more I tried to be different from you without identifying with you, the more I unconsciously adopted the parts of you that I did not like. I absorbed and became that which I was trying to be rid of. Before I could join with you and truly receive your love with no obstacles or fantasized expectations, I had to learn to both identify and separate from you.

Healing for me has also meant becoming accountable for my own life. You are not responsible for filling my aloneness. To truly begin my spiritual journey I had to feel my aloneness for myself. I had to let go of the childhood fantasy that I had a magical father in my life that could take care of my every need and save me from every crisis.

The causes of my strongest anger allowed me to give up this "magical" thinking. I always expected financial help from you and when you did not give me all the money I thought necessary to help me through graduate school, I felt angry and betrayed.

I had to go through that hardship in order to stand on my own two feet. It was not easy to let go of the all-mighty, all-knowing, fantasized father I wished you were. I was angry at you for not saving me every time I fell. That anger was part of grieving the loss of the fantasized father. Knowing more about your life and your father has been helpful in letting go of the fantasized father. Seeing your humanness is somehow very healing. It helps me to give up my childhood dream of you being "magical" and me being dependent.

Human Son, Human Father

To heal I had to make you mortal,
human in every regard.
I had to acknowledge your shadow
while not seeing darkness as all you were.
I had to make the good in you real,
I had to identify with this good.
I had to see how I am like you,
and own that I am me.
I had to see how I am different from you,
and own that I am me.
Only then could I claim completely who I am,
and only then
could I truly be free to change and grow.

Sometime soon I would like to go back to my hills in Tiburon, and I would like to take you with me. I would like us to lay on our backs together and feel the moistness of the earth beneath our bodies. Maybe we could lie head to head and do a little "cloud shaping" together. I have some secret places in those hills, and those hills have some secret places in me. I would like to take you there. As the grass blows over our faces and we touch, maybe a new kind of father–son magic could fully enter our lives, a magic that is real. A magic that will be with us long after we have left our bodies. A magic of the spirit. A magic that is unconditional love.

I love you,
Lee

Dear Lee,
For sure, I would like to take you up on your invitation to visit the Tiburon hills and share in your secret and treasured

places. There are no words to express my appreciation for stripping yourself of old defenses and sharing with me your most intimate thoughts and childhood secrets. I want you to know that I really hear you. It is important for me to hear how your expectations of me were not met and to experience the pains and wounds of your childhood. I remember there was a part of me that wished I had a magic wand and could magically wipe away all your pain and hurts and make everything all right again.

As I watch you shed more of your outer armor and defense, I find also that I allow myself to feel your heart and your vulnerability. I feel closer to with you than I ever thought possible. It also stimulates me to go back and try to remember some of my unmet expectations with my father and share those with you. Hopefully, this process will help both of us to not be stuck in the past, to heal the past, and move on with a new, healed, and a loving whole relationship with each other.

As I read what you wrote about your "fantasy" father, I was reminded of my own struggles with my dad, your grandfather. When I was about five years old, Mom and Dad opened a retail store in Long Beach, California, selling dried fruit. It was located on Atlantic Avenue between Broadway and Third Street.

I do not have very many specific memories of my father during those early years. I do remember that our house was on an alley behind the store. My parents worked long hours. They opened the store at 7 AM and did not close until 10 PM. They did this even though they rarely had a customer in the early morning or evening hours. We ate dinner at exactly 5 PM and finished by 5:15 PM. Each day my parents would rotate who would eat with the kids.

Up to age six, I did not think that there was anything my father could not do. I knew he loved me and I trusted that he would always be there for me. I could not imagine my father lying about anything.

About this time, I was in the store one day when I saw my father put dates into a flat that was marked 50 cents a pound. Then he put the same dates into a flat that was marked $1 a pound. I was puzzled and asked my father what he was doing. He smiled and said, "People always think they are getting something better if they pay more for it." "But Dad," I said, "that's lying." He became very stern and brusquely stated, "That is not lying. That is business. And don't ask me any more questions."

Well Lee, I remember my heart breaking. The person who I thought I could trust, who would never lie, and who was perfect, was not that person at all. My "magical" expectations that he could do no wrong were crushed. It took me many years to recognize that my father was human like everyone else. He had frailties and weaknesses and he was not perfect. In regard to my dad's fatherly role, I also began to see that if I had received the same parenting as my dad received from his father, I might very well have behaved in precisely the same manner. I think that I, like so many others, grew older and looked back and saw that my parents really did the best job they knew how in parenting. Our parents are limited by the traumatic experiences they had as children with their own parents. Perhaps if we had the same parents as they, we would have behaved the same way with our children.

One of my first memories of my father was at the dinner table in the kitchen. With every bite of food I took, he would insist that I have a whole piece of bread. Each of us ate almost a whole loaf of bread at each meal. I remember my embarrassment when I went away to college and I was compulsively eating a whole loaf of bread at each meal, while others stared at me in disbelief. I learned later that when my father was a young child on the farm in Russia, his parents poured as much starch as they could into the children because there just wasn't that much other food to go around.

My mom ran the show and was the boss of the whole family, including my father. I didn't think of this as unusual until I was about seven or eight years old. There was a lot of verbal fighting between my parents all through their marriage. My mother had a tremendous temper and a very sharp tongue. In those days I tended to side with my father. I felt sorry for him. Even as a kid, I wondered why he didn't stand up to Mom and why he seemed so weak. Mom was the disciplinarian and the "man" of the house. She would frequently slap me on the face. There was a strap in the kitchen and Dad was directed by Mom at specific times when I needed a strap to my bottom. Now that I think about it, getting whipped and eating in the same room does not make for a great association.

Like you, I wished my father had been stronger and less fearful and had stood up to my mom. In reading your letter there is a terrible gnawing in the pit of my stomach as I recognize my part in recycling this pathology from one generation to another.

I remember my father liked to garden. He would start avocado trees by putting the avocado seed in a cup of water. He also grew gourds. And he loved to water and take care of his lawn. I think that when he was doing those things, he was the happiest. It is no accident that in my later years, gardening and being outdoors have become some of my greatest joys. That is one area where I identify very closely with my dad.

My memory of my father during those early days was that he was a gentle soul who usually had a soft and peaceful energy. I remember that Dad was very unmechanical. Mom kept him under a tight rein. He seemed like a child and would not do anything without Mom's permission.

I remember that one Thursday night a month my mom allowed him to go to the wrestling matches at the Municipal Auditorium in Long Beach. He would cheer on his favorites and boo the wrestlers he didn't like. As I look back at it, this was a pretty healthy outlet for him. He seemed to have no other way of letting go of all the anger he had stored up inside. It seemed a far better way of handling his anger than letting go of it on others.

I loved Sunday afternoons because occasionally we would go together to the minor league baseball games Dad cherished. This was always a special treat for me. I remember going on vacations to Lake Henshaw and my father teaching me to fish. And I remember with pure joy the occasional Friday nights when the whole family would go fishing on Belmont Pier.

Dad kept his feelings to himself. I wonder what his inner dialogue might have been. If I asked him questions about anything, his response was, "I don't know." Later, when I was teenager, I would ask him questions about his own feelings. He would respond with, "I don't have any feelings. There is nothing to talk about." Dad pouted a great deal and attempted to get my attention by getting me to feel sorry for him. For many years I chose to identify with this trait. During your childhood, I can remember pouting and having people feel sorry for me, so they would not get angry and attack me.

There was no television when I was young. But Dad kept the radio going at all times. He listened primarily to the news and would hear the same news over and over again. In later years I began to think that he did this so he would not have to listen to the inner voice of his own feelings.

Lee, I have never before tried to group my thoughts together about what my fantasized father might look like. As an adult I guess I have done my best at just attempting to accept my father as he was. I have had scattered thoughts, but I don't remember trying to organize them together. So I find writing about my fantasized father to be quite an exercise in both pain and learning. I remember when I was 14 years old, wishing my father was husky, strong, and athletic. I wished that he had been more mechanical and able to fix things around the house when something went wrong, like some of the other fathers in our neighborhood.

When I was 16 years old I was an usher in the Long Beach Theater. John Wayne movies played there for two or three months at a time. I ended up knowing the key lines in the movies, and walking and talking just like John Wayne. The fantasized father I wanted then, although I am still embarrassed to admit it, was John Wayne. (I now thank God he was not.) I wanted my real father to be many things he was not. I wanted him to be strong and decisive. I did not want him to be a weak and afraid.

I wished we could have talked together, which he thought he could not do. I wished he could have been happy and not overburdened by life. I wished that my father had been a good verbal communicator so that he could have found other ways of expressing himself without his more typical reactive behavior. I wish he had not been a workaholic and had spent more time with me and more time in nature, which I believe he loved.

I wish that he had not been so fearful and believed in the power within him. I wish that he had not, with such regularity, given all of his power away to my mom, myself, and others. I wish he hadn't been so compulsive about time, another trait I copied.

It would have been my desire that he could have gotten off the treadmill of life and learned the holiness of being still. I would have liked to have seen him recognize that there are other things in life besides working so hard. I wish he had not sacrificed so much of his life for the sake of his children's future. I wish that he had more zest for life, had been more totally alive, and more willing to take risks.

The father I wanted to be for you and Greg was a father that filled in the empty spaces I thought I did not receive from my father. I wanted to be an unconditionally loving and uncritical father who was also a strong male figure. I know that in my own way I loved both of you more than anything in the world, but I was also a fault finder. I think there was a sick part of me that wanted you to do well to make me look good as a father.

I wanted to be honest about my feelings and share them with you. I wanted to make time for you, not because I thought I should, but because I wanted to. Obviously I was not very successful at meeting those goals. I wanted to be a cuddly father-bear figure for you—a father who was wise and would have the right answers or would tell you how to find them. I wanted to be able to teach you what honesty, integrity, trust, and dependability are all about. I wanted you to know that my love would always be there for you. I wanted you to know that helping others is what I thought life was all about. Yet, all this time I was having great trouble loving myself.

We both know it is very difficult to give your love to others if you are not seeing yourself as lovable.

I wanted to show you a marriage where the father and mother were loving and caring and not arguing so much. I wanted to share my strengths with you, but I also wanted to share my weaknesses. I wanted to demonstrate that it was possible for a man and a woman to live with each other as equals. I wanted to demonstrate for you the absence of abuse of any kind. Unfortunately, for much of the time you received just the opposite picture.

I wanted to be a brave father. I remember a couple of years ago I shared my true feelings about being the first passenger to fly with you after you obtained your pilot's license. I admitted how frightened I had been. I remember your response: "Dad, it's not a matter of fear. You were just plain stupid! I was only 18 years old at the time."

I suppose in a way, I have attempted to list here my wishes and fantasies about the kind of father I wanted to be. I wanted to take on what I thought was positive in my own father and reject all I thought was negative. We both know, only too well, that I am not alone in having those good wishes—and then to wake up one day with the awareness, "My God, I am doing it just like my father, repeating all the negative things that I said I would not."

I ended up being a full participant in a marriage that was very similar to the one that my dad and mom had. As the marriage went on, you and Greg were witnesses to our arguments and verbal abuse. It was the very thing I was determined would not happen when I became a father.

I must confess that I have a split memory. Part of me can say I was a loving and devoted father who looked forward to being with you and who went to and enjoyed nearly all of your activities. Another part of me reminds me that I was drinking every night. Although I wanted to believe I was there, I was not really emotionally accessible to you.

As you mentioned in your letter, my priorities were frequently upside down. While you were growing up, I, like my father, was a workaholic. I had a sick kind of pride: I was either in the hospital or seeing my first patient at 6:30 AM and often would not get home till 6:30 or 7:30 PM. I remember loving to read to you when you were in bed, but I wonder how much energy I had for you after such a long day in the office.

As I said before, like my father, I spent a lot of time pouting when things did not go my way. And when things would go bad, my back would go out. That made people feel sorry for me. It was hard for others to get angry at me when I was in such pain.

I guess we both know that regardless of how organic your back problems may seem, there may be, unfortunately, similar psychological dynamics that you learned from witnessing my episodes of back pain. Hopefully, as we clean up our unfinished business with each other and heal our relationship with our own fathers, we can put a stop to recycling this intergenerational guilt and fear.

In my days as a child psychiatrist I would be loving, kind, and understanding with my patients in my office, but when I was home I could become the opposite. I was like my father. He was very pleasant with his customers in the store, but two minutes later in the house he could be a totally different person.

In spite of consciously wanting it to be different, I think one of the reasons so many of us end up becoming just like our own fathers is that we still have a strong unconscious drive to please them by becoming like them. We hope that if we are like them, they will approve of us. My unconscious wish to identify with my father was much stronger than my wish to identify with the male hero I fantasized him to be.

It is as if our unconscious thinks that if in some magical way we become like our fathers, we can become one and the same with them. Then at last, our fathers will finally approve of us, be proud of us, think of us as just like them, and then will love us forevermore.

Love,
Dad

The Wish for the Perfect Father

As a child I (Lee) wished my father was perfect, but in time I realized he was flawed. Now I know that there is no way either of our fathers could ever have fully satisfied our needs. Even the most attentive and loving of fathers could not possibly attend to or satisfy all the conscious needs of a son. Therefore our fathers could never satisfy our vast unconscious needs.

When our fathers failed to meet our needs, we began to fantasize about the father we wished we had. We looked at our neighbor's dad and wished ours was more like him. We saw movies and wished that Dad could be a little like the bigger-than-life heroes we saw on the screen.

We were probably like most boys—less in touch with any emptiness within and more in touch with the many images of what we wanted our fathers to be. This process is natural for a boy. At some point, every boy wishes his father was different.

Imagination

As a child I (Jerry) found imagination to be a wonderful treasure. As an adult I have found, when used in a positive manner, it has the power to heal and take my creative energies beyond anything I might have thought possible. Similarly, I have found that when I have used my imagination in a negative way, it can limit me as I fixate on fear.

Like many children, both of us (Lee and Jerry) had very active imaginations. We each remember creating fantasies to lessen the loneliness we carried around inside when we felt unwanted and rejected.

Many boys do what we did. When boys don't experience a loving father figure, they imagine one who wants to be with them all the time. The fantasized father loves to play with them and finds it fun just being with them.

When I (Lee) was young, I remember imagining that I had a vicious lion whom everyone was afraid of. With a magical wand I would tame this creature and he had to do everything I said. In many ways the lion represented my father. Through my magical world of imagination I could secretly control him. I could punish him. I could even kill him, then bring him back to life. I could even make him into a cuddly teddy bear.

There are so many little boys who grow into men having lost sight of the boundary between what's real and what's imagined. They are adult men who are still playing childhood games. But to them it is no longer a game—it is reality.

Before a boy consciously asks the questions, "Who am I? Why am I here? Am I any different from my father?" he is already unconsciously seeking the answers and a meaning in his life. At both levels, the boy will continue to search for what it is to be a man and what it is to be a human being.

When we were growing up, Dad and I had distorted images and fantasies about what it is to be a man. Boys' fantasies are fed through all-powerful, dominant and controlling images. Many boys identify with the images of a Superman or Rambo. Boys with a dominant, abusive, or absent father, may yearn for qualities of kindness, tenderness, and patience. For this we have television's Mr. Rogers.

Much of my (Lee) healing with my dad began when I realized that my fantasized father had never been a realistic image that Dad could have lived up to. Many movies and children's television programs seem to reflect the unconscious process of the fantasized father. Few, if any, are balanced images of a man. Can you imagine a father with a personality of both Rambo and Mr. Rogers? On one hand we recognize a need for balanced images for our sons. But it would be naive to believe that an absence of unbalanced images would alleviate the natural need for a son to have images of a father who is larger than life.

The Internalized Father

Problems arose for each of us when we unconsciously clung to the fantasized father in our adult lives. Certain aspects of the fantasized father became a part of us; we internalized them. The internalized father is a conglomeration of how our father was, what we wanted him to be, what we heard from others about our father, and our cultural beliefs about fathers. For us, as with many adult sons, this internalized father ruled our lives. The healing of our relationship really blossomed when we saw that the image of the father that we created within ourselves may be quite different from who our father is or was when we were young.

It has been important for us as adults to begin to feel the emptiness and the pain that was created during our childhood.

When we kept our pain and emptiness hidden from each other, it frequently came out in self-destructive ways. Hiding our pain from ourselves interferes with becoming whole men. Our relationship with our internalized father needs to be healed before we can be truly free. Until we addressed our emptiness, we failed to see the image of the father we had created in response to our emptiness and yearning.

Many men, like us, are never able to have the qualities that our internalized father says we should have. When the fantasized father is internalized we often overcompensate for what we thought our father lacked. I (Lee) will always try to fix something—even if it takes many hours. As a kid I always fantasized that my dad could fix things, that he wasn't all thumbs. I have found that as long as I tried to acquire what my father lacked, it was hard for me to embrace his positive traits.

Through talking to each other and other men, we have both been amazed at how aspects of the fantasized father become internalized, inhibiting our ability to be happy and fully functioning adults. Redefining our internalized father has helped set us free. This freedom has been a result of working through the pain of our past relationships with our real fathers. By so doing we have been able to begin directing our minds to adopt a healthier image of our relationship and of what it means to have a father and be one.

The healthy internal image of father can become a truly positive force in our lives. It can become a voice that embraces our wholeness and our humanness, and recognizes that we are all teachers and students to each other.

For years we both were stuck in the old patterns of our critical internalized father—until we chose to consciously create a different image within ourselves. When we weren't willing to explore and heal our relationship with both our real and internalized fathers, we continued to have a difficult time finding happiness in life. We now both listen to the positive internalized father. We needlessly carried the negative internalized father for many years. For far too long those beliefs dominated our existence. That is not to say our negative internalized father never comes out in our consciousness, but when it does we are far more willing and able to work through it, instead of letting its critical voice dictate the truth about who we are.

Positive Internalized Father

The following list includes some of the key qualities of the positive internalized father:

1. I discover what it is to be a man by letting go of the past and asking myself who I am in the present moment.

2. I am lovable and capable of giving love. I am safe. I need do nothing to prove myself worthy.

3. I am human and have faults and make mistakes. I accept this.

4. I am powerful and can make a positive difference in the world.

5. I know that God (or a higher power) is with me every moment wherever I go. I am not abandoned.

6. I have choice. I am responsible for my happiness and can direct my mind to peace.

7. I know that feelings are appropriate and part of being a man. It is okay to express my feelings to others. Vulnerability is not a weakness.

8. I am gentle with myself. Judgment and self-criticism only injure me and lower my potential.

9. I do not have to please other people in order to feel good about myself.

Negative Internalized Father

Here are some qualities associated with the negative internalized father:

1. I deny my pain and act as if nothing ever has or ever will hurt me.
2. I blame everybody else whenever things don't go well. I act as if blame is how you get rid of shame and guilt.
3. I don't ever make mistakes. And even if I did I'd never admit it. Mistakes are a sign of incompetence and weakness.
4. I avoid vulnerability and never let my guard down. I compete with other men and make sure I win. I have only competitive relationships with men.
5. I believe that if you fail to live up to your father's expectations and wishes, you are inadequate.
6. I avoid looking at my own faults and insist on being right all the time.
7. I like to control other people.
8. My motto is please everyone, but pretend it doesn't matter.
9. Nobody is worthwhile unless they win, achieve, succeed, surpass, and conquer.
10. I am always tough, critical, and hard on myself. This is what will make you a man.

The Unhealed Child Within Fathers and Sons

For years intimacy was a foreign word to us. Both of us had elaborate and similar ways of protecting ourselves from intimacy. If others didn't fit our mold, we promptly rejected or criticized them. We frequently felt that the purpose for other people in our lives was to fill our needs (in reality our wounded child's

needs) and offer us immediate gratification. If immediate gratification was not forthcoming, we were not above punishing
the "guilty party." We are both sad to say that for a long time
many people were uncomfortable around us because they were
never quite sure what our behavior was going to be.

When our wounded child went unrecognized and unhealed
we tended to be very opinionated and dogmatic—especially
with each other. We would demand that everyone else fit our
expectations and that things be done our way. It was okay for
us to yell and scream but it was not okay for anyone else to act
that way. Things were always black or white. In those days if
you asked us about our feelings toward each other we would
have acted as if everything was fine.

For years we both denied that we had any authority problems, although there was much evidence to the contrary. Initially
we failed to see any causal relationship between ourselves and
our fathers. In time we were able to explore our relationship
with each other. As we did, we were able to see that as children we frequently suffered from feelings of guilt. It was as if
we had done something wrong that caused our fathers to reject
us. In our conversations with each other we have found that
as children we both had painful periods when we felt unlovable.

As adults there was still the same frightened child inside us,
causing us to feel that we were unlovable. Though it comes
easier now, we both have had difficulty in the past expressing
feelings of intimacy, love, and tenderness—especially to each
other. We have had tough times in our relationships with both
men and women. For years we could not see that so much of
our behavior was a result of an unhealed wound. We continued to carry it around hidden from our conscious awareness.
We denied any pain—especially to each other.

There were years when I (Lee) thought that there was no way
my relationship with my dad would ever be healed. In fact, I

was convinced that my anger was justified. I really did not want to give it up.

I (Jerry) had so much guilt about so many things, about being a father, I thought I could never let go of it. A part of me believed I deserved to be punished. Though Lee's and my relationship is not free of conflict, we have made great strides in healing. If we can do this, there is definitely hope for other fathers and sons.

The first step for us was to have a willingness to go inside and explore the pains and the hurts of our childhood that had been kept for so long under lock and key. We began to openly look at memories we had repressed. We needed to experience our anger and tears before we could let go of them. As a result of our healing journey, we have become freer and more empowered to be who we are.

It is important to recognize that a father or son need not be alive or available to undertake this journey with us. Though it is wonderful when both parties are available, it only takes one mind for healing to occur.

There is an increasingly new readiness in men to embrace the unhealed, frightened child within. For men today, this important task includes facing one's inner pains, sharing one's innermost thoughts, and becoming comfortable with intimacy. As more men learn to do this, their relationships with each other and with the women in their lives will become more honest, equal, and authentic. It is through the necessary healing of our past wounds that we can begin to have healthy and whole relationships in the present. It is through this profound process that we can learn to banish our fear of intimacy and recognize our need to accept the love of others and, ultimately, to offer our love unconditionally to all those we encounter.

THREE

Father Substitutes

Freedom occurs the moment we let go
of all our attachments.

I do not want my children to have a monolithic memory of me.... On the contrary, I would like them to know the vulnerable man that I am, as vulnerable as they and perhaps more so.

GEORGES SIMENON, *MAIGRET'S MEMOIRS*

Dear Lee,

I remember when I was around six years old, I began to develop the belief that I was an accident and not a planned baby. I believed that I was unwanted extra baggage that my parents had to carry around; I felt that I must have gotten mixed up at the hospital and was actually someone else's baby.

In 1993, three of my cousins came to hear Diane and me give a talk. During lunch a conversation about my mom came up. One of my older cousins stated that when I was born my mom went over to her mother to explore the possibilities of exchanging babies. My mom wanted a girl and believed they wanted a boy.

At first I thought this information was a joke. I didn't want to believe it. Then I didn't know whether to laugh or to cry. I began to realize that perhaps some of my abandonment fears were not all my imagination, but were based on some fact.

During my childhood and much of my adult life, I usually felt like an outsider, like I never really belonged to the group. Not being clear who I could identify with and trust, intimacy turned out to be a life-long problem for me.

I had confusion about male and female identification from the very beginning. My dad was the one who nurtured. He was more tender, soft, gentle, outwardly loving, accepting, and supportive than my mom. Mom played more of what would then have been considered the male role. She was the power and the disciplinarian. She made the decisions.

I had long curly hair like a girl until I was 4 years old. I think that it must have taken years for my mom to accept that I was a boy. Any amateur psychologist would say that I must have had gender identification problems right from the very start of my life.

My dad was always around physically. If not in the house, he was in our store right in front of the house. Despite his physical proximity, he was usually silent. However, one of my first memories of Dad was a very powerful and loving one.

I was about three years old and we had just returned from a Sunday afternoon ride. I had fallen asleep in the back seat of the car. I remember Dad holding me in his arms and taking me to my bed. My eyes just barely opened before shutting again and I remember having the thought, "My father will always be there to hold me, love me, and take care of me."

As my childhood years passed, it was painful to discover that this was not always going to be true of my dad. However, at 55 I realized that my memory of that event was a symbolic memory of my trust, faith, and belief in God.

Although I have identified with my father's gentleness, there was another part of me that did not want to be someone who looked weak, indecisive, and allowed my mom to make all the decisions. Although it is not easy to admit it to you, in my teen years I wanted Dad to be like Charles Atlas, the Arnold Schwarzenegger of my time.

As I look back, I can see how my brothers acted as father substitutes. As you know, Lee, my two older brothers were six and nine years older than me. In many ways they turned out to be very positive role models.

They answered a lot of questions that my dad was not able to answer. They gave me guidance when my dad had nothing to say. In a sense, they coached me and helped me to find my own answers and solutions. And like good fathers, they saw value in my potential when I thought I had none.

They helped me learn something about accepting many of the things I found difficult to tolerate in and out of our home. They were role models for how important education is and how essential it is to be highly motivated and disciplined in the art of learning. They taught me that if you work hard enough, nothing is impossible.

On the other hand, they were not above ordering me around and criticizing me. By observing their nonverbal communication, they reinforced what I had already learned from my dad: "At all costs, do not show your feelings. Find some way of stuffing, repressing, or denying your feelings in order to stay in control."

Everyone in my family seemed smart. I went to the same public schools as my two older brothers. They did great in school. I had many of the same teachers as they did. This made things difficult for me because the teachers were always comparing me with my two very intelligent brothers.

Even before going to school I felt clumsy and dumb. The worst happened when I flunked kindergarten and had to stay back a year. Not knowing anything about being dyslexic until years later, I was devastated. I did not know the meaning of the word "self-esteem" at that time but I'm sure that mine hit bottom. I was not very athletic. I had no male teachers to identify with until I was in the eighth grade. At the tender young age of five or six, I already felt lousy about myself. I felt unlovable and unloved.

As an adult, I continued to seek out father substitutes. Though loving, my dad was meek and certainly not a powerful leader. Today I am certain that having some father substitutes helped me develop my strength, and taught me to be of service.

Of all the teachers that I have had, one stands out as a supreme father figure. During my internship in 1949 at the United States Public Health Hospital in Brighton, Massachusetts, I found him in a place I would have least expected it.

My internship was a rotating one. The service I was most fearful about was the time I had to spend in surgery. The chief surgeon's name was Dr. Howard Fishburn. I will never forget him.

Somehow we formed a father–son relationship. He gave me the gift of refusing to see my clumsy past. The idea that anyone could entertain the idea of such a clumsy person assisting in surgery was beyond all reason, I thought. I have to say that as a kid and as an adult, I was always known for my clumsiness. The few times I tried to carve a turkey, it would invariably end up on the floor.

Dr. Fishburn saw something in me that I was never able to see in myself—someone who was competent and had an unlimited capacity to learn. In the area of surgery, he gave me the gift of self-confidence. In my wildest dreams I would not have thought this possible.

In this internship, the most an intern could do was assist the surgeon by holding retractors and cutting sutures. To my utter amazement, Dr. Fishburn soon had me doing appendectomies and other surgical procedures. I was the one who used the scalpel and he was the one who assisted me.

All through my internship, Dr. Fishburn tried to talk me into becoming a surgeon and staying on at the hospital in a surgery residency. I was one of those rare people who went to medical school with the idea of becoming a psychiatrist. Many instructors at Stanford Medical School tried to talk me out of that.

Dr. Fishburn was not attached to my answer. He lovingly accepted my decision. This man loved me and touched my life in a way that no man had previously. He helped me open up my heart and my mind. I began to believe in myself. This was like magic to me; the things I had once thought impossible were suddenly possible.

•

If a father figure is someone you look up to and respect, who teaches you that nothing is impossible, who is a model for how you would like to be when you grow up, who accepts you just as you are, who loves you with all his heart, who will always be there for you with love, and who forgives you for all of your many mistakes, then you and Greg have become father figures for me.

You and Greg have helped me accept myself. You have helped me let go of the guilt of my past. You have moved from having a very tense relationship with me to having a most loving one. I can imagine no greater gift.

I have been your father and you my son; yet in some ways you have fathered me, and I have been your son. In many ways we have become closer friends than I ever thought possible.

> Love,
> Dad

Dear Dad,

Your letter allowed me to see and experience the frightened child within you. For most of my life I have somehow overlooked this part of you. It seems that I rarely think of you as a child. I believe this is true for most sons. I have known very little about your childhood, and even less about your childhood wounds. I have tended to see you as either incompetent or over-competent, either somebody I would never want to be or somebody I never could be. Seeing the vulnerability of a child within you allows me to experience you and myself in a different light.

Most of my life I approached you from my frightened, needy, and angry child. When I did not or could not get from you what I thought I needed, I looked around for father substitutes. In my life some of these have been positive mentors (teachers, coaches, and grandfathers). Others have led me further into confusion about manhood (drug dealers, critical men, and macho men).

Because I have so unconsciously identified with *my* wounded, frightened child when I am around you, I have rarely been able to see *your* childhood wounds. I have often been like an infant with you and expected that all I need to do is cry and you would (and should) be there to take care of my needs. This infant has no awareness or thought of your needs or wounds, only an awareness of the need to be taken care of. In reading your letter I became aware of how, even as a grown man, I have often overlooked the frightened, injured child within you.

In the days after reading your letter I realized that in the past I learned to treat other men in ways similarly to the way I treated you. I overlooked their wounds, repressed mine, and ended up with no close male companions.

As I think about it, this is how the search for father substitutes begins. This is not necessarily a negative search, for we need to be able to have our wounded child noticed and cared for by another man, if not our father. However, I am aware that for me the search has been so deep and so long, that I have overlooked what may be able to heal me.

I believe that as I am more open to healing and listening to your wounded child, mine will also be healed. I also know that this will allow me to be closer to other men.

Dad, sometimes I am able to best express my innermost feeling in poetry. This poem is for you.

I Want to Love, Not Just Need You

I realize that I have continued being a child with you.
I have wanted you to give to me,
and whatever it was, I have wanted more,
and however much it was, it was not enough.
In my spiritual path I have practiced non-attachment,
and yet with you I have always practiced wanting and
    never getting.
Can it be that I am afraid of you, of your love?
Was I starved as a child for nourishment from your love?
I don't remember much about intimate times with you.
Did we have them?
I remember fishing trips and baseball games but I don't
    remember
embraces and closeness. Was it there and I forgot?
Sometimes I feel I am still wanting something from you
but I don't know what it is.
It is a hunger that occurs without knowledge of the food to
    fill it.
I have looked to father substitutes, but to no avail.
The food is now in front of me.
Healing our relationship attends to an ancient hunger
    within me.
I no longer need to look upon the past as an empty plate.

Dad, I have been so concerned with getting my needs filled
(and never really looking at what those needs are) from you
and many father substitutes, I have not focused on loving
you just for *you*. I want to love you, to love some more, and
to love deeper yet.

When I was a child I would look up to the stars and wonder how far the universe went. It was my first experience of
infinity. Since having children I have found myself wonder-

ing how far love and compassion can go. As I look into my children's eyes, I ask myself, How fully can I love? I am met with the experience of infinity once again. There is no end to the depth that I can love them. When I am loving deeply and completely, I know there is even more available. Love is endless in its depth.

Somewhere in the infinity of love for my children lies more healing of my relationship with you. As I see more of your wounded child emerge, I have the same experience of loving you as I do with my children. Isn't love remarkable? It knows no boundaries and knows no time. Who would have thought that a child born in 1925 would be loved by a man born in 1957? Thank you for letting me love the child within you. It helps me to love the man who raised me, the man to whom I now write this letter, and myself.

In your letter you wrote about how Grandma's treating you as a girl caused some confusion for you. It brought to mind some aspects of my own sexuality and how you and Mom related to me. When I was growing up, I only remember one conversation with you about sex, and none about what it was to be a man. All boys need guidance in becoming a man. Consistent with our culture, you left this up to nonverbal communication and the distorted portrayal of men on television, in the movies, and in *Playboy* magazine.

You described how Grandma under-emphasized your male identity, and how you were left feeling as though you should have been a girl. I never felt I was supposed to be a girl. However, with your lack of direction or validation of my maleness, Mom's attempts at validating my maleness felt inappropriate. From Mom I felt that there was something "special" about me being a boy. Though she never intended it, this became very uncomfortable for me. When a boy's maleness is only validated by a woman, something vital is missing in his development of self.

When I was about ten, I fell on the crossbar of my bike. I hurt my testicles and came into the house doubled over in agony. Mom reacted almost hysterically. I think she must have thought that I had cut my balls off or crushed them. I never got the same reaction to injuries on other parts of my body. I doubt that she meant it that way, but the message I received from Mom was that my genitalia is the most important part of my body and represents who I am. The message that I got from you about sexuality was vague and ambiguous.

Discovering my maleness through the father substitute of my mother has led me to repeat my search for validation from women. In my twenties, I endlessly looked to women to validate and notice my maleness. I avoided bonding with men. Sex, using the "equipment" that says I am male, became a primary way of experiencing being a man. This caused me to overlook the depth of what it is to be a man and the importance of intimacy. I also did not see the fundamental importance of deep male relationships.

You mentioned how your brothers were both positive and negative father substitutes. The same was true of my relationship with Greg. On one hand, as my older brother he showed me what was possible. He was always athletic and popular with boys and very popular with girls. He always seemed self-confident. On the other hand, I always compared myself to him. His body was always stronger and more muscular than mine. I never felt very good with girls, and was always kind of shy. I was never as good athletically as he was. Greg never rubbed any of this in my face. He was always kind. He was proud of me and I liked that. But deep down I felt I never measured up.

As an adult I enjoy athletics a great deal, and have actually discovered that I can be pretty good. One of the many forms of athletics that I enjoy now is going to the gym and working out with weights. I have also been a long-time student of martial arts. Although I enjoy these, and know that on many levels they are good for me, I can't help but wonder what first attracted me to them. Was I trying to have the muscular body Greg always had? Did I want to be sure I could physically handle any situation to compensate for all the years that I felt Greg could beat me? I would like the answer to these questions to be an enlightened and emphatic "no." However, I am quite sure that most of my twenties were spent trying to measure up to my successful brother.

As I look back at my relationship with Greg, Mom, and you, I realize I have put up my guard all too often, rather than let myself feel your love. At other times, I have become angry and emotionally distant and protected myself by disappearing. I thought I could treat my life like the pieces of a pie, keeping relationships apart and unhealed while not affecting the whole of the rest of my life.

Dad, healing our relationship deepens my purpose in life because it allows me to love more fully. I hope that on my last day on earth, I love more fully and deeply than I did the day before. If I do, I will have fulfilled my purpose.

> In gratitude for being my
> father and my teacher,
> Lee

As It Used to Be

It has been extremely helpful for us to develop an historical perspective for understanding how the experience of being a son has changed over the years. This has helped us see how our own roots, cultural perspectives, and societal beliefs have affected us. In the process, we gain some understanding of how social expectations and roles have shaped our relationships.

Imagine you could listen to a great uncle from the early 1900s, describing his father–son experience.

I was born in 1910. I began working with my father at a very early age. It was expected. It seemed natural for me to follow in my father's footsteps and I never thought of doing anything else. I knew quite clearly what the future was going to be.

I always knew that I was there to help Dad. The work ethic was very strong. Family survival was the priority. There were very few choices. For the survival of the family, everyone knew that they had to work together. It was a work relationship I had with my dad. I was never really in touch with inner feelings. In fact, there was never any discussion of them. Psychology was in its infancy and not yet part of the popular culture.

I knew that when my father became too old to work, I would replace him as the provider of the family. I knew that there would come a time when I would take care of my father in his old age.

There was great division between masculine and feminine work. My dad taught me the ways of manhood and fatherhood that he had learned from his own father. There was always real respect for authority. What was thought to be right and wrong were made very clear. It was as if rules for my behavior had been painted in giant letters across the sky.

There was almost no room for tolerating any misbehavior.

No ambivalence in my mind was allowed. Like most men of his time, my father was unbendingly strict with me. But compared to my sister, I was the chosen one. My dad taught me that men were the wise, strong ones, the decision makers. They were where the power rested.

I remember my dad had pride in being a man. However, his was perhaps a narrow view of what it was to be a man: who was the strongest, who could do the most work in a single day, and who could be the better provider.

Although there were advantages to such a defined role, it was not without cost. What did I really learn and how expensive was it? I learned that it was not at all right or acceptable to talk about my fears. It was okay for girls to express emotions, but if I did I was considered weak. To be a man meant to deny my emotions or any part of myself that could be considered feminine. I never really questioned that my role was to be just like my dad.

If I wanted approval from my dad, I kept my feelings to myself. I buried my feelings so deeply within myself that I ended up feeling nothing.

Religion was important only as a Sunday affair. For the most part, there was no carry over into our daily life. There was not much tolerance for differences. If people were not your color, religion, ethnic background, or economic class, they were simply not accepted.

When I was a young man, sons tended to learn from their fathers that men were first-class citizens and women were second-class citizens. I grew up believing that women were supposed to be submissive and to hide their intelligence. Women were not allowed to vote. They were expected to cook, clean, and take care of the babies. In no way were men to help with these woman chores.

This man's story suggests that sons had a clear external image of the father, but did not have a clear image of the real man *inside* the father. Consequently, they didn't know the real man inside themselves. These historical generalizations aid in understanding male cultural roots. In many respects we are not that different. Times have changed dramatically, but generational beliefs and wounds that need examining and healing still remain.

History of Abuse and Rage

In the healing of our anger and rage, it has been helpful for us to see where our distant brothers and fathers came from. There are scant records, but we speculate that for many generations there has been an overwhelming amount of physical, emotional, mental, and sexual abuse. Probably, as in our father–son relationship, many boys have witnessed a Dr. Jeckyl and Mr. Hyde syndrome in their fathers. They saw their fathers as one kind of person in the home and another kind of person outside the home.

Did sons in those days learn to genuinely respect and trust their father's authority or were they simply obedient out of fear? Both of us have found that we developed internal rage when we were covertly told by our fathers, mothers, and our culture to deny and repress parts of our selves, our manhood, in its wholeness. Often we became ashamed of who we were. Our shame became projected onto others.

As we claim who we are as men and acknowledge our history of verbal abusiveness, we have begun to heal our shame and guilt, and become less abusive to others and ourselves.

Then as now, sons were prone to be publicly or secretively competitive with their fathers. Many learned from their fathers that children and women are kept in line by physically and/or emotionally controlling them. When sons became fathers, they did the same thing. And we are the distant but connected sons of those men.

What is a Father?

Fatherhood is a role in life that has high expectations and many assumptions, but little or no education, support, and guidance. As we have searched for a better understanding of our pursuit of father substitutes, it was helpful to explore, both together and individually, what being a father means.

As you can see from these letters from two men of different generations, the role of men and fathers has continued to change in society. The women's movement helped women explore their individual identities and their roles in society and the family. Inspired in part by these explorations, and in response to the changes resulting from the women's movement, each of us has had to reexamine the roles that we automatically accepted in the past.

Pioneering family therapist Carl Whitaker once wrote, "Parents have only one choice. They get to choose how they want to be wrong." It has been important to be easy on ourselves as we explore being fathers. Having a sense of humor has lifted us above strong temptations to criticize. No one does a perfect job of being a father. One of our favorite cartoons shows a banner hanging over the stage of a large auditorium reading, "First Annual Convention for Children From Functional Families." Only one person sits in the audience.

Before trying to capture with words what a father is, it is important to acknowledge that the true experience of the father goes beyond language. We have each discovered in profound ways that our need for the father is deep within us, a yearning for connection that is as deep as the need for breath.

Father hunger, the yearning for connection with the father, is no less demanding. From this hunger we have searched for father substitutes. This is equally true for women. Father hunger and searching for father substitutes also occurs at the spiritual level. We (Jerry and Lee) are on conscious spiritual paths and yearn to experience our connectedness to a higher power. Sometimes we have repressed this and have looked for substitutes for God. For us, the most reoccurring god substitutes have been money, power, and control. It has been very central to our healing to recognize that none of these is ever satisfying and a hole in the soul remains until the father–son relationship is healed.

In our culture and media, fatherhood is portrayed in so many different and inaccurate ways that it is virtually impossible to define what a father really is. To some, the purpose and usefulness of a father stops after the delivery of sperm. To others, the purpose is little more than to be sure that food is on the table. Many men we have spoken with deny their pain and anger toward their fathers by saying, "My Dad always took care of the family. We always had food on the table and clothes on our backs. He was a hard worker and a good provider." During hard times in our history, such as the Depression, many courageous fathers continued to take care of their families despite great hardships to themselves. In many ways, these men were the heroes of their time for their commitment and tenacity. At the same time, we should not try to deny the wounds in the son that arise when the father is absent. Being a good provider and protector can be part of being a father, but by no means all a father needs to be for his son.

Then what is at the heart of the father's role? For us, it has been helpful to know what we strive for in being fathers. It has been important in our healing that we ask for help in areas where we are having problems. It has also been enormously helpful to discover what we missed as children. Usually what we missed we have had difficulty giving.

When we ask adult sons to describe how their fathers raised them, we usually hear about the negative aspects. This is not to say there are no good fathers, for indeed there are many. But it is clear that there are countless sons in pain because of what they did not receive from their fathers. In the following list, we describe how fathers can strengthen their sons, using phrases that men have shared with us in our workshops. We've also provided a second list after this, listing ways that fathers undermine their sons.

How Fathers Strengthen Their Sons

- By expressing love physically and verbally.
- By teaching healthy ways to express anger and pain, as well as joy and excitement.
- By encouraging them to develop emotionally, physically, intellectually, and spiritually.
- By helping them build self-esteem.
- By demonstrating a willingness to be wrong and make mistakes.
- By protecting and being courageous, but acknowledging being afraid.
- By being reliable and teaching about trusting ourselves and others.
- By demonstrating male vulnerability, warmth, and sensitivity.
- By setting appropriate boundaries in exploring the world, and by appropriately disciplining.

- By honoring and respecting both male and female sexuality, and demonstrating a respectful, equal, and loving relationship with their partner.
- By demonstrating cooperation, conflict resolution, and teamwork.
- By demonstrating the capacity to forgive.

Realistically, no son has consistently received all this from his father. But it is the absence of these qualities that brings about father hunger, and then results in the search for a father substitute.

How Fathers Undermine Their Sons

- By having high expectations and making their love and acceptance of their sons conditional, according to how they fulfill these standards.
- By being emotionally explosive or distant.
- By criticizing and believing that nothing is good enough.
- By being afraid to admit mistakes and having the need to be right all the time.
- By being either macho or weak.
- By being physically absent, isolated, and/or unreliable.
- By encouraging competition and being controlling and judgmental.
- By being afraid of true feelings.
- By degrading and manipulating, or being victimized and controlled by women.
- By holding grudges and prejudices.

The chasm between this list and the one preceding it is where the search for the father substitute is born. Deep wounds are

often created, yet the fear of emotional pain keeps us from looking within.

Fear of Pain

As we became willing to heal our relationship, we found that
two things were very clear.

- We started out with feeling a painful distance between us.
  We had tremendous pain and anger as a result of this distance, but these discomforts remained unconscious.
- We also found that the feelings of alienation were less threatening to us than confronting our pain.

For this reason we were very tempted to continue turning
our backs on the idea of creating peace. For years we chose
the predictable pain of the past, allowing it to repeat itself in
the present; we avoided risking the unknown, uncontrolled
experience of our emotions. We had been afraid of the process
of healing, which is to say we were fearful of love and letting
go of past grievances.

Both of us thought what we had to say would be too much
for the other person to handle. Our fear of inflicting pain on each
other kept us from sharing our desire for a closer relationship.
To our amazement, working through the pain *with each other*
has been one of the most freeing experiences of our lives.

Today

We feel very fortunate that we have both been willing to heal
together, but healing can take place whether the father or son
is present or not, alive or dead. Peace and healing require only
one mind to be willing to forgive, to no longer hold onto the
past. Healing has nothing to do with changing the past. It has

to do with healing our own thoughts of the past, letting go of grievances, nurturing our own injured fearful child. Only then can we know the freedom we find by taking responsibility for our own feelings, actions, and lives. For us, healing has meant coming to the awareness that there is no time for, or purpose in, finding someone to blame.

Father Substitutes

Like fathers, father substitutes are rarely all positive or negative. In our lives, some father substitutes have genuinely and compassionately served us on the path of becoming a man. Others have primarily hindered the process and thrown us into deeper confusion, longing, and despair.

One of the most important points we want to share is that our healing was initiated by recognizing and experiencing the yearning we had for our fathers. This included exploring how we looked to father substitutes for support and guidance. This process has required being open to whatever comes up, including our repressed anger and sadness. By working through this, we were able to begin healing our relationship together.

It has been important for us to realize that building healthy new father–son healing our relationships are not dependent on anybody changing. No one needs to become the perfect father—or the perfect son.

Coming Together

As we observe the world today, both of us are saddened by the number of fatherless sons we see. We find a world filled with boys and men hungry for the love of their fathers. All too often, they sadly remained starved for a love that never comes, that they will never allow into their lives.

Fortunately, we have also been uplifted by the number of men we have found who are reaching out from their hearts, not only to their own children, but to other children as well. In creative and authentic ways, these men are attempting to father more responsibly. It is not an understatement to suggest that our social, ecological, and global future depends on more men healing their father wounds. When we fail to heal these wounds, we frequently repeat our fathers' worst errors. This is true whether the father was a part of the family unit . . .or was never there.

Particularly as children, we model ourselves not after what people say, but what they do. In many communities we have visited, over three quarters of the homes are lacking a father. In those homes where there were fathers, only a few were said to serve as positive male figures. This is a sad commentary indeed!

Growing boys desperately need models with whom they can identify. There are organizations that have been around for a long time, such as Big Brothers, which are doing a wonderful job in this area. There are also a number of new organizations where men are devoting a tremendous amount of time to serve as role models for boys. It is a new opportunity where a boy can learn trust and dependability.

With 25 million, or close to 40 percent of all American children in fatherless homes, communities need to join together to create solutions that responsibly meet the emotional, psychological, and spiritual needs of fatherless sons. There are too many communities today that are simply not making our children a high priority.

In the increasing number of men's groups exploring men's relationships with each other, women, and the planet, it is time that some focus be given to finding ways to be of service by reaching out to fatherless sons. It is our hope that men, individually and collectively, will take a renewed interest in raising today's sons, who will become tomorrow's fathers.

Though these challenges are daunting and complex, at the risk of appearing naive, we do feel there is a simple answer. We believe with all of our hearts that no problem faces us in this world that can't be solved with love. We believe that regardless of the question, regardless of the challenge, love is *always* the answer.

FOUR

The Hole
in the Soul

*To surrender to love is to not be desirous
of anything, except the giving of love.*

When a father cannot—or will not—love his son, his lack of love creates an emptiness. There is a place in a son's heart that can only be filled by his father. When this special place is empty, the son is left to believe that he was not loved because he didn't deserve to be.

———————————

DR. ROBERT ACKERMAN, *SILENT SONS*

Dear Dad,

Yesterday I was thinking how wonderful it feels to be healing our relationship. I like having a father. This has been a very long time in coming. On a deep level I have always wanted a father, but during my adolescence I didn't feel satisfied with our relationship. As I look back, I think it was a combination of your not being very available and my distancing myself from you. Curiously, the joy that comes from developing a relationship with you now allows me to remember how deeply I missed you then. I never allowed myself to fully feel my longing for you. In fact, as a teenager I would have said "Who needs you?" Yet the truth is I felt there was a hole inside me.

It pains me to remember all the ways I denied this yearning and unconsciously tried to fill it. I believe that I yearned for both a deeper relationship with you and also with God. In our home I did not have the language or the support to deepen either relationship. For years I searched for ways to fill the void.

I began using pot in junior high, and alcohol and cocaine in high school. For ten years, beginning at age thirteen, I received narcotics from the medical community for my faked back pain. By my late teens and early twenties I was turning to drugs to fill any type of inner yearning.

During high school I often felt like a failure. I wanted to please you but was never sure how you felt about me. In college I was afraid of relationships and painfully shy; because I also felt like a failure, I thought if I buried myself in my studies both problems would be solved. I went through four years of college in just under two years and graduated with honors. This was the start of my attempting to fill that hole within me with accomplishments in the world.

The list of how I tried to fill the void is sadly long: Money, success, women, adrenaline rushes in risk-taking activity, sex. It is not with blame that I tell you all of this. My purpose is not to raise guilt in you. Regardless of what has occurred, I know that I am responsible for my own actions. I share this in order to heal myself and hopefully spark healing in others.

I had to realize I had a hole within. For years I filled it with things that only made the longing worse and my sense of hopelessness more persistent and pervasive. I truly believe that when a strong father–son relationship exists, our external searching is minimized.

Many people never experience this as children. The good news is that it is never too late. I am glad you are alive and willing to go through this with me. However, I also believe that even if you were not, I would still be processing and healing at this stage of my life. The letters that I write to you would be useful even if there was not a father to send them to. I also have an internalized father—a composite of you that my mind made up. Writing these letters helps me with that internalized father as well.

I would like to share with you an experience that reconnected me with the hole within.

Recently I went camping at Big Basin State Park. Lexi was about nine months old, and as usual, she woke early. I put her in her little baby carrier and we set out on a hike just before dawn. Magnificent redwoods were shrouded in morning mist from the ocean, highlighted by moon-lit darkness. As dawn approached bringing the new day, I felt full and very fortunate to be where I was with my beautiful young daughter.

We came across a tree that symbolized much of my life. It was just as tall as many of the other trees except something was quite different. There was a huge hole in one side, big enough to walk in. Inside the tree, looking up, I was amazed to find that it was hollow. I could see the early morning sky one hundred and fifty feet above me.

My heart sank as I realized that this hollow tree was me much of my life. In late childhood and early adolescence, I seemed to grow like everyone else on a physical level, yet inside I felt hollow and empty. In looking back I feel that the emptiness was often more of an existential void, a knowing that there was something more, a yearning for a connection with you, and a longing for a connection with God.

In our family there did not seem a place or words to express this. I remember discovering poetry at a very early age. I think this was the closest I came to a vehicle to express myself. Eventually I filled the emptiness with things that could not satisfy me but gave the illusion that they did.

In college and graduate school I discovered the world of spirituality. I became fascinated and involved with a variety of Eastern traditions and developed a meditation practice. Yet to some degree, my hollowness persisted. I was still like that empty redwood, reaching to the heavens with an emptiness inside.

Healing my relationship with you is part of my discovering my substance within. I now experience more substance within myself, even when I am experiencing an existential emptiness. I never felt substance and emptiness simultaneously, but they certainly can go together. I think that healing my relationship with you, including processing all the anger and pain, is part of my spiritual path. I no longer come from a place of emptiness to be filled by God, but rather from fullness to experience God. These words seem to be contradictory, but as I write them they make perfect sense: It is the discovery that I am not empty that fills me. Experiencing my fullness is what replenishes me.

Ironically, since I stopped wanting and expecting you to fill me, I feel much fuller. My acceptance of who you are, your life, and our life together, allows something magical to occur. The acceptance of father allows the acceptance of Father. Healing the battle with father stops the battle with Father.

In closing, I would like to share a poem with you:

Roots and Sky

I lay beneath an ancient redwood tree,
awed and comforted by his life.
For hundreds of human lifetimes
he has reached into the earth with his roots,
and stretched to the sky with his branches.
Age and wisdom live in his roots,
innocence and purpose in his new growth.
His grandfather and father stand nearby,
whispering with the wind.
He will grow beyond them,
but take some of them with him.

His roots intertwine with his fathers and grandfathers,
nourished from the same source.
His branches reach to the same Father in the heavens.
Father and son meet once again,
drawing from the same universal source.

I am as my friend the redwood tree.
You, father, are still a part of my roots.
I feel you standing close by.
When you no longer stand,
my roots will still mix with the soil
that once supported and nourished you.

Beyond all of our past conflicts and differences
you and I are the same.
We reach into the earth with our roots,
alongside our fathers and theirs before,
and we reach to the sky to become One with our Father.
I now realize that I cannot reach to the heavens without
strong roots.
Turning my back on my roots inhibits my ability to heal.
Without healing there is no new growth.

Love,
Lee

Dear Lee,

My heart was very moved by your last letter sharing your poem and your reflections about the hole in your soul. I am so grateful to learn more about your thoughts and feelings when you were a child.

My memories and perceptions frequently don't match yours, but that is not to say that mine are correct and yours are wrong. It simply means that they are different.

My memories conflict, even for myself. It seemed to me that your mom and I were very outgoing in sharing and demonstrating our feelings of love to you. Yet during the last years of the marriage, you were witness to much conflict between your mom and me, with an atmosphere of fear, empty of love.

I remember that I could be quite strict, demanding, and I am sure unloving when trying to get you and Greg to clean up your rooms and get better grades. At the same time, if you had come to my office, you would have found it cluttered and messy. You are quite right that in many ways I was not there for you physically or spiritually. Particularly, during the last months of the marriage, I remember being torn between wanting to come home to be with you and Greg and not wanting to come home for fear your mom and I would end up in another fight.

I thought we encouraged discussions about feelings, but I have to admit that since I was not in touch then with many of my own feelings, they were never shared with you. You learned from me since I handled my feelings by stuffing them inside and not revealing them even to those closest to me. That most certainly contributed to creating a hole in our relationship.

Lee, as I try to remember my childhood, it seems from a very early age I believed something was missing in me. Many times I felt what was missing was intelligence. I had many of the same teachers as my brothers and I got lousy grades while they received good ones. I remember trying to joke about my pain, telling others that my brothers got the "intelligence genes" and I got the "personality gene."

I, too, really didn't get to know what was going on inside my dad. The hole I felt was like the empty feeling in your stomach when you are very hungry. I think I have spent a good deal of my life trying to fill that hole. I tried to fill it by pleasing people and trying to get them to like me, even though inside I felt I was a failure and disliked myself very much.

I tried to fill up the hole by writing professional papers and obtaining recognition from my peers. But the hole still remained. I found that material things didn't really bring me lasting happiness, which only increased the pain I felt. Yet I also felt that life had to be more than the struggle I found myself in. There was a hole in my heart and I didn't know why.

I tried to hide how empty of happiness I felt during the last part of our marriage. I wanted people to think I had a successful marriage, and I wanted to perpetuate the lie that I had it all together. I did not want anyone to see the empty hole in me.

It was not until 1975, when I was 50 years old, that I began to get a hint of what that hole was all about for me. I had consciously started my own spiritual journey. It was not long after I heard Mother Teresa say that the biggest problem in the world was spiritual deprivation.

She went on to say that spiritual deprivation is when you feel empty of spirit, unloved, unloving, and feel no capacity to love others or oneself. That description fit me like a glove. In 1975 I began to realize that I had been suffering from spiritual deprivation most of my life. I had felt separate, disconnected from God, and had gone through life using guilt, blame, and self-condemnation as a way of life.

As I have continued my spiritual pathway, I began to experience my purpose here to be giving, to love and forgive, and to let go of the fearful past. As a result, I no longer experience the hole on a daily basis. I have realized that the hole I thought was always there was really my denial of my connection with God.

Well Lee, when you were growing up you witnessed all the symptoms of the hole. I lived a compartmentalized life. My life was going at 300 miles per hour. Although I fooled myself into thinking that you and Greg were my top priority, my work actually became the top priority and everything had to fit around that. I see there is more healing to be done because I am getting a pain in my stomach just putting this down in words and facing those experiences once again.

My joy is that you are willing to reach out and face the

pain, express the pain of the past and then hold onto it no longer. I am sure it will enable us to feel whole again and remember more of the joy and love that we once experienced with each other.

Love,
Dad

P.S. Recently there was a party at the Center for Attitudinal Healing and I met a woman who shared with me the following story: When you were in high school some 20 years ago, you had a party one night in my office without my knowledge. People there got drunk. Her son came home inebriated, with a book he had swiped from my office, *Love is Letting Go of Fear.* His mother said she read the book and it helped her immensely in what was going on in her life at the time. Lee, maybe there are no secrets and there are many mysterious ways in which the past comes back to us.

Symptoms of the Hole in the Soul

For years we experienced an inner yearning. Given a voice it would have said something like this: "There must be more to life than this. There is something missing and I don't know what it is."

Regardless of how successful we were in our lives, this feeling of emptiness persisted. We found ourselves financially successful, having wonderful people around us, wonderful kids, and plenty of activities. Still, there was that gnawing feeling that there was something missing.

The symptoms of the hole in the soul vary but they may be as simple as feeling angry and irritated at the world. It can be feeling depressed and not knowing why.

We found the hole in the soul to be spiritual deprivation. It is a condition that came into being when we were feeling separate from God. At times in our lives we ended up believing we were totally unlovable. Writing this book made us realize that for so much of our lives we carried feelings of loneliness. We also realized that at the times of greatest despair we were not even remotely conscious of this state of spiritual deprivation.

In the depths of our unconscious there was a state where we felt separate from our father and our Father. For years there was a part of us that tried to deny that we were longing for either. On one level, we discovered an emptiness in which we missed a soul connection with our fathers. There was a longing for bonding with the very essence of our fathers, but the real person within our fathers often remained a mystery.

On a still deeper level, we discovered a hole in our soul that came from our missing God. On the deepest level possible our souls were hungry for spiritual fulfillment. This hunger asks to feel the peace of God once again, and feel connected with our creative source and each other. It is a desire to experience being home in the heart of God.

Filling the Hole by Trying to Be Different From Our Fathers

The hole within ourselves, created by our struggles and yearning for our fathers, has flavored every aspect of our lives. We found that many of our internal and external conflicts were the result of trying to heal, complete, surpass, or repress our relationships with our fathers by over-emphasizing other areas of our lives. Examples of this for us have been in the areas of career and marriage.

In our conversations we found that in our twenties and early thirties we both believed that ignoring and/or going beyond our father had the greatest importance. We believed that if we were in a successful marriage and had a successful career, then our father issues would cease to be important. Once we gave ourselves time to look within, we found that despite these achievements, there was still something missing. Even as adults, we longed for a relationship with Dad that went beyond the surface. In the past our fear, anger, denial, and emotional complacency kept us from healing our relationship, and so for years the hole in the soul remained.

Culturally we have only a vague idea of the role of the father. We are left on our own to figure out what it is to be a father and what sons need from our fathers. I think that many sons do what I (Lee) did. I vacillated between being proud of my Dad to the point of idealizing him, hating him to the point of making him the cause of all my problems, and devaluing him to the point of ignoring him altogether.

Once we allowed ourselves to look within we discovered a deep desire for union with the father and the Father. We found that for many decades the only thing that we consistently did, though not always consciously, was try to be different than our fathers.

For years we deceived ourselves with the belief that if we made ourselves different from our fathers we would not need to address our emptiness. As we each began to look into the hole within us, at times the pain was psychologically overwhelming. What we yearned for was connection, but the wounds seemed so deep that we often lost hope. While writing this book we both had moments when we wondered why we were subjecting ourselves to all this when it would be so much easier if we just continued to ignore it.

In our minds, we had created endless lists of why healing could never happen and how we wanted to be different from our fathers. We discovered the following cycle kept us from even starting the healing process:

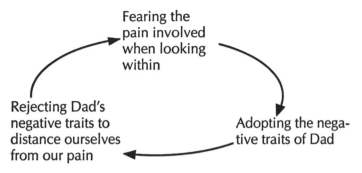

The Hole Within

There is a peculiar psychological truth that many men, including us, have experienced: The more we try to be different from the aspects of our fathers that we don't like, the more we end up imitating them.

This cycle of desiring to be different and then imitating is pervasive and cross-generational. I (Jerry) never wanted to adopt my father's emotional distance from his sons or his passivity with women, but at times I found myself doing both. I (Lee) never wanted to adopt my dad's passivity with my partner, but I have to really fight being a "yes man."

Though for years our inclination was to distance ourselves from the negative aspects of our fathers, we found that to heal we had to do the opposite. We found a willingness within ourselves to do our best to know who are fathers were. In my (Lee's) case, I also needed to be willing to discover who my father is today. This process was healing for us because we discovered our fathers' humanness, and moved beyond just seeing them as machines that disappointed us. This is not to say we liked everything we found, but we were able to move toward acceptance and away from judgment. This whole process was also difficult because we needed to embrace the vulnerability within us that still deeply yearned for our fathers. Instead of pushing away we needed to pull closer.

There's a Hole in Me

Each of us experiences the hole in a slightly different way. Sometimes it is during our darkest moments or in a heartfelt piece of writing, such as a poem, that we are able to get to the essence of this hole. In the following excerpt of a letter Lee wrote to Jerry, we see an example of this.

Dear Dad,

As a child, I don't recall ever feeling really whole. Instead I felt a hole. I had a hunger but didn't know what would fill it. It is impossible to fully capture my experience in words. When I try to write about it, even now, I regress into feeling a tightness in my chest that is black with sadness. This constricted sadness was my companion for much of my early life. It is not that I didn't have fun like other kids, or feel that you and Mom loved me, it just seemed as though something essential was missing.

As a kid I never asked myself adult questions like "Who am I?" As I allow the child within me to emerge now, this is what I hear:

The Search for Identity

Who am I?
Am I the list of things that you, father, want me to be?
Am I the things that I run from?
Am I the vast emptiness that emerges
when I no longer have an answer
to the question: Who am I?

Am I the sensitive boy that Mom wants me to be?
Or am I the darkest of my dark thoughts
at any given moment?

You and Mom were married until I was 15. Many of my memories of you involve you going to work, coming home, and drinking. I knew that I needed you, but I didn't know how to speak of my need. These words now emerge:

Somehow I know that to discover
the full breadth and wonder of who I am,
I must explore who you are and who we are together.
As my father, you can be the chains that shackle me
to illusions and mediocrity
or the doorway to my self . . . and the decision is mine.

I need to make peace with you in order to find me.

Healing my relationship with you
is like putting up the sail on a boat.
I may have no wind,
but without the sail
I would sit adrift when wind did arrive.

The Three C's: Comparison, Competition, and Competency

Like us, many men struggle with their feelings about being competent. As a result we see endless competition in the male world. At various times in our lives, each of us practiced the opposite of a common saying "If you can't beat them, join them." Along with our fathers, we practiced "If you can't join them, beat them."

Both of us have tried to find self-acceptance through achievement. We invented the world's tallest ladder to the sky. Its rungs were infinite in number; they never ended. As soon as we grabbed hold and pulled ourselves up, another rung would soon appear. We were forever climbing and never arriving.

This ladder came from the false notion that in our male world the way to competency was to prove that we were better than the next guy. It came from the false notion that if we were not better, we were incompetent.

The three C's became locks on the door through which we must all pass to find peace of mind. A vicious cycle of competency, competition, and comparison ruled our lives. We would compare ourselves to others (usually males). When we were "better than," we would feel superior; when we were "less than," we would feel inferior. This inferiority/superiority complex always left us feeling separate and never at one with anybody. Whenever we felt inferior, we would enter some kind of competition, usually in our own mind. "If I am better than him," we would say to ourselves, "then I will be competent and no longer inferior." Once we felt "better than," then the whole comparison cycle would start again.

Like most men, our relationships with our fathers provided a lot of fuel to keep this cycle going. I (Lee) have often vacillated between wanting my father's approval and wanting to prove I was better than him. Neither position left me feeling love or oneness with him. My dad would tell me and others how he was dyslexic and not really bright in school when he was growing up. Though not his intent, this often left me feeling hopeless and angry. I thought that my father was brilliant and competent, and in many ways felt I would never please him or be as competent. If he wasn't bright, that meant I was really a hopeless wreck. In high school I felt incompetent and hopeless, and essentially gave up. In college I overachieved and felt that if I did not do perfectly I was not competent. Both behaviors—giving up and overachieving—left me with the same feelings of not belonging and not being competent.

Tasting Our Lives

Someone will ask us to taste something they are cooking. They will ask if it has enough spice or the right blend of herbs. Upon tasting, it is clear that something is missing. Despite our knowing this, it is still difficult to say exactly what's missing. We can describe our experience of what we taste, but fall short of knowing what the *soup* needs.

We have found in our journey together that our attachment to anger and guilt kept the holes in our hearts empty. We had a love/hate relationship that kept the true essence of love from filling our hearts. With so much guilt and blame, the spirit of love and forgiveness had no room to flourish.

When we believe there is no one to blame and can at last share our vulnerability with each other, the pains of the past and the holes in our souls begin to be healed. Healing begins when we see that our happiness is not dependent on the behavior of others—now or in the past.

PART TWO

The Wound

One of men's greatest resources for change is our wound and our longing for the missing father. We can heal ourselves by becoming the kind of fathers we wanted but did not have. Create out of the void, out of the absence.

SAM KEEN, *FIRE IN THE BELLY*

FIVE

The Frightened Little Boy in the Adult Male

*One of the most important things in life
is discovering the innocent child
still existing inside each of us.*

In remembering dad's love, however buried or unexpressed, we reclaim a disowned part of ourselves: the one that wants to love and be loved.

SAMUEL OSHERSON, *WRESTLING WITH LOVE*

Dear Dad,

In your letters and our recent conversations, you have been willing to show me a side of you I rarely saw while growing up: your fearful child within. When I was a youth, I always saw you as competent and believed you had the world by the tail. As I recall, your fear or my fear was never discussed. It has meant a lot to me to see you as a mortal man with fear. Seeing you in this new light has further opened my heart to you and enabled me to see how many of my fears are very similar to yours. It is amazing how even though we never talked about your fears, I adopted so many of them. Indeed communication between father and son goes far beyond words. I never knew how important it was for a father to talk to his son about his fear as a child and how he still is fearful.

In response to the fearful child within you, I would like to write directly to your inner child. As I write to you, I am also writing to the fearful child within me.

Dear Frightened Child in Jerry,

I am sorry that it has taken me so long to notice you. I have also been afraid. Regretfully, my fear has kept me from being able to see your pain. I want you to know how precious and dear you are. You are truly a magnificent child. I know how hard it must be for you to live with your controlling and dominating mom and your successful brothers. I know how much you yearn for assertive, gentle, and compassionate direction from your dad.

Part of me wants to make excuses for your mom, but the truth is that I believe she was abusive to you. I can't imagine what it must be like to live a childhood wondering if you are in the right family and never really being allowed to be a kid. I imagine that your mom always wanted a little girl. Being the third boy must not be easy. Also, your mother constantly calling you stu-

pid is not right. I want you to know that your mom's actions have nothing to do with your worth. It is okay to be a little boy, and it will be okay to let yourself become a man. Your brothers are brilliant, and I can imagine that you are proud of them, though you also can't stand following behind them—always being compared and perceiving that you aren't as good.

Please know, Child Jerry, that you are a light to the world and have a great deal to offer. You are a child of God and not a mistake. You are here because you are supposed to be here. You have a right to be who you are, including being male. I want you to know that I care very deeply about you. I realize that I have ignored you for years, but my heart is now open to you. I don't want you to be afraid to be with me.

In the past I have been afraid to be with you. In a fantasy, I wanted a father that would always be there and always be strong. This left little room for you, the wounded child, to be there. Now I truly want a father who can be with me. I now know that for you-as-father to be with me, I must be willing to be with you-as-child. I will do my best to nourish and honor you, God's child. Thank you for trusting me enough to let yourself be seen after I ignored you for all these years.

Love,
Lee

It is probably good for me to be writing this letter now. I am afraid in my life. I have a lot of faith that everything is going to be good and that God is in my life at all times. However I have also had times lately when I wonder why I should go on. I become afraid.

I am not really sure why I felt so alone. Right now "why" doesn't seem important. I am just tired of having that same aloneness rise up inside of me as an adult. I would like to share some of what I am going through. As I do, I want to acknowledge that much of what is happening is resurfacing the fearful child within me.

At this moment, it feels that I have not and will not ever be successful in an intimate relationship with a woman. My fearful child alternates between blaming myself and blaming everybody else, including you. Consequently, I can't seem to find much peace right now.

Six months ago, if you asked me how everything was I would have told you enthusiastically how wonderful my life was. I would have told you that I was in a happy marriage with a wonderful woman, loved being a father to my two daughters, and was enjoying my successful practice as a psychologist.

Then my wife Carny began to voice her hidden unhappiness with our relationship that, because of her fear, she was previously unable to tell me. Today she doesn't know if she can continue with our marriage. I have become aware of how blind I have been to much of my intimidating and controlling behavior. I am hurt and feeling guilty for not recognizing her pain years earlier, and remorseful for being critical at times—things I probably learned from you and Mom.

The child within me feels very alone. I feel like I can't do anything right and no matter what I do, sooner or later I will always be left alone. The pain of a possible separation and the effects this would have on my kids causes my pain of your divorce from Mom to resurface.

During your divorce I was angry, afraid, and felt responsible. I felt abandoned and pretty unlovable. This is exactly how I feel now. I wanted to support Mom and help her through her pain, yet I was also angry with her—about what I am not entirely sure. This is just how I feel toward Carny. That fearful and guilty child is still very much a part of me. Despite all the therapy and inner child work I have done, my inner child still fills me with sadness and longing, and he doesn't always know what to do with his anger. I have felt rage and felt guilty every time the rage has surfaced. Again, this is just like when I was a kid.

About the same time all this began with Carny, a previously diagnosed inner ear neurological condition progressed and I began to lose more of my hearing. Ultimately, I had to make the difficult decision to limit my private practice. This affected me in a number of ways.

The child in me has never really felt that I was enough. Being successful, both monetarily and in helping other people, kept this part of my wounded child hidden. Now I find myself feeling as though I have failed. I was attached to being a good provider as part of being male. Intellectually I know that I will not go broke and I feel that things will work out. But fear is in my face and it won't leave me alone. I am not sure how I will provide for my family and this scares me.

In my meditations and more centered times, I realize my hearing loss is manifesting for me what I was afraid to do. For many years I have envisioned my ideal lifestyle as teaching, writing, and lecturing, with plenty of time to spend with my kids. This is now my exact schedule. The difficult part for me is getting out of the "I have to" place and into "I choose to."

At this moment I am far from centered. It feels that life is happening to me and that I am a victim of myself and the world. I want my life to be like it was, and yet when I am honest with myself, I can see I really needed change. I just pray Carny can find her way back to the relationship and we both develop the strength to work on ourselves. The good news is that Carny now has the courage to be honest with me. The bad news is that it is very painful to hear what she is saying and she feels it may be too late.

We have been doing couple's therapy. In those sessions she has told me some things that are very difficult to hear. She has told me she has been pretending to be happy in the relationship for some years; that it is easier for her when I am not at home; that she is not sure that she can ever be in love with me again.

I know that she has been wounded and has come to this point partly because of me. When she tells me these things, hurt and rage are mostly what I feel inside. I think much of this is because it takes me back to my childhood feelings. I had a secret fear you and Mom pretended to love me, but deep down loved Greg more. I always felt he was better at just about everything and anything you said to reinforce me was more because that was what you were supposed to do. When Carny talks about pretending, the child within me gets his old fear reinforced: "Lee, you are unlovable and if people say they love you, they are really pretending."

I always thought it would be easier for everybody if I was not there. During your and Mom's divorce these feelings were pervasive. I thought that both you and Mom were ready for different lives that did not include having a teenager around the house. I felt that both of you were more interested in your new relationships than me. So when Carny says she finds it easier when I am not at home, all my old child fears and wounds come to the surface. I want to be angry that she isn't able to love me like I want her to, yet at the same time I feel very unlovable. Right now I am not really aware of the anger. I am just in a lot of pain.

I truly don't think Carny is doing anything wrong. She is taking responsibility to find herself and what she wants. I know she needs to do this if we are to have any hope for a happy marriage. Yet I cannot even begin to tell you the fear, guilt, and pain that surface in me when I think about what is going on—and I seem to be thinking about it all the time. I am sure that through this process I will have the opportunity to do some healing of my inner child. I am not sure how you can help, but I know that it is important for me to share this with you.

I can see that we are both grown men with wounded fearful children within us. We both have already done a lot of healing work, but the fearful child is still within us both. Maybe working on our relationship is part of the healing we have not fully completed. The one thing that I am grateful for is that we are both willing to share our wounds with each other.

In peace,
Lee

P.S. It is now several months later and I have just reread this letter. I am no longer in that dark, confused place. I have found this period in my life is teaching me so much about loving, releasing, and just plain living. I have had some of the most difficult days in my life this year, yet I have also had many of the most centered and consistently spiritual. I am grateful for both.

Dear Lee,
My heart aches for what you, Carny, Jalena, and Lexi are going through. Please know that Diane and I send to all of you our love and compassion. I know full well that it is not your intention to make me feel guilty, but it is difficult for me not to feel twinges of guilt once again. It is tempting for me to think that if I had been different, maybe you would not have the challenges you are now facing.

Your letters, revealing your vulnerability and sharing your innermost being, continue to touch the very center of my heart. We are father and son, yet in another sense, we write as equals. We have become spiritual guides for each other and our age difference has disappeared. Thank you for nourishing my inner child.

The difficulties you and Carny are having at this time trigger many old feelings for me. Many of these, I must admit, are ones I'd rather forget. But I know this would not be helpful for either of us now. Perhaps by my attempting to go back and look at what happened when your mother and I were separating from each other, both of us can find some healing.

Though it happened over 20 years ago, I still remember my divorce as one of the most painful periods of my life. It is my recollection that I stayed in the marriage for as long as I did because I thought I was protecting you. It was my impression that as things were getting so much worse, I came to the conclusion that I was doing you more harm than good staying in the marriage. I don't know if you remember, but there were a number of separations before the final one. Greg had gone to live in Lake Tahoe, I think to get away from the marital turmoil. I felt sorry that you were trapped in it.

As an aside, as far as treating you and Greg differently, you are quite right that I did respond differently. You were both so different. There was no way I could treat and love you the same. I did feel that my love was equal for both of you. In looking back, I feel there was less pressure on you than on Greg. He was the first child and your mom and I were much more anxious about our first born, not knowing what to expect. If there was favoritism, it is not in my awareness. I wouldn't be surprised if Greg feels that you were the favored one, but frankly, I have never asked him.

Following the separation and divorce, it is my memory that I wanted you to be with me and I missed you terribly. There were other times when, I am sad to tell you, it felt good just to be alone. I am sure that you must have received a lot of mixed messages from me. It was just awful being alone and not being with you the first Thanksgiving and Christmas after our separation.

As you share more about the challenges in your marriage, all that old pain not only comes back to you, but it also comes back to me like a nightmare. I would like to think that I have rid myself of all my guilt, but it continues to reappear. I am not as consistent as I would like to be and I do vacillate. There are days I feel that I have rather successfully completed the work in healing the fearful injured kid in myself. There are many days when the fearful kid is no longer around. But then there are still days when that fearful kid pops up again like a jack-in-the-box, telling me I have more healing work to do.

Lee, as I try to recapture some of the early memories about my fears as a child and take another look at the fearful child within, it occurs to me that I had an inexhaustible list of fears that followed me into my adulthood. When I wrote my first book, *Love is Letting Go of Fear*, I remember asking my mom about her fears. She replied, "I am convinced I have more fears than anyone else in the world." And I thought to myself how much I had identified with my mom in my life.

When you were young I wanted you not to carry around fear, so I tried to look fearless. For a long time I carried around tons of guilt for not being the "fearless father" model I thought you needed. I consciously wanted to be the opposite of my father whom I saw immobilized by his fears. And then one day I woke up to discover that I had become the same kind of father for you that I had.

I used to think my fears were hereditary because my dad and mom had so many of them. They had a fear about this, a fear about that, and they seemed to be constantly worrying about something. My memory of them was not that "the best is yet to come," but rather, "the worst is yet to be."

As I have shared with you before, it was my impression that their philosophy was "yesterday was awful, today is horrendous, and tomorrow is going to be even worse." I was brought up to be a very obedient son and I was quick to make their philosophy my own. I guess I can say that I came by my fears very honestly.

It was my impression that my dad and mom believed fear was the most important ingredient in life. It kept them awake and alert to all the bad things that could happen. Not to be fearful was not to be fully awake and responsible. To be fearful is what kept you alive and helped you react quickly and decisively to any unanticipated situation. My parents felt being a pessimist made rational sense and was actually healthy. To them, half a glass of water was always half-empty, not half-full.

Although it is still my belief that my parents had more fears than most, I do believe that many people in their time had similar feelings about the value of fear and worrying. I remind you that I was born in 1925, just before the Great Depression when the stock market fell and many people were out of jobs. It was a time when the future looked bleak to almost everyone.

As I remember him, my dad was always a very cautious man. He was definitely not a risk taker. It seemed difficult for him to make decisions and he seemed to always rely on my mother, not for just major decisions, but for all decisions. In retrospect, there were times when I wondered if not wanting to make decisions and take responsibility for them was my dad's way of avoiding feeling guilty if things went wrong. I would describe my dad as a man who had extremely low self-esteem, who was filled with tremendous self-doubts and inadequacies, but always had the strength of a survivor.

I do remember my mother belittling him frequently in front of me, calling him "dumb" and "stupid." These were words that were later applied to me both in and out of the family. Unfortunately they were also words that I began to apply to myself. With this as a brief background, let me see if I can be successful at sharing some of my fears.

I remember that I was afraid of the dark. I was afraid the "bogey man" would come and attack me at night. I was afraid of what I could not see. I was afraid of being alone.

My mom liked to go shopping and would take me with her. She was afraid of becoming lost. I then became afraid that I was going to get lost in the maze of people in the department store. We went shopping all of the time because Mom would almost never keep anything she bought. She was constantly trying to return items and demanding her money back. As I became older I was unfortunately assigned this task.

While shopping, Mom would frequently leave me with Dad to wait for her. More often than not, she would not come back at the time she said she would. My dad and I would get panicky thinking that something bad had happened to her, or that maybe she would never come back. It seems like there were abandonment fears in every aspect of my life. These fears stayed with me long into my adulthood.

I remember I was always fearful I would say the wrong thing. There was a time when I stammered. In class I was fearful of raising my hand and saying the wrong answer. I was deeply afraid of being ridiculed by other people. So I stopped raising my hand, even if a part of me thought I had the right answer.

To say that my parents were very strict would be the understatement of the year. Perhaps they were the ones who invented the word "overprotection." For example, when kids my age would be outside playing in the vacant lot next door—

climbing trees or playing marbles, hopscotch, cut-the-pie, or cowboys-and-Indians, or simply being pals and talking with each other—I would only be allowed to watch.

I was not allowed to go out and play. My parents' attitude was that I was fragile, like an egg that would easily break. I remember my sadness and depression as I would sit on the chair in our bay window watching the other kids play in the empty lot across the alley from where we lived. I wondered why my parents were so mean and uncompromising about giving me the freedom to risk having friends. I continued to suffer deep loneliness. I felt awful at being so different. After not being allowed to be one of the regular guys, I started to believe there was something wrong with me and I would never belong.

I grew into an adult who looked self-assured on the exterior, but on the inside I constantly felt I didn't belong. I felt different from others and never experienced being totally accepted by anyone.

My mother had a terrible fear of water and was always afraid I was going to drown. I think that I pleased and relieved her by accepting her fear as my own. There was a time I was fearful of elevators and high places. I was fearful of people not liking me and talking behind my back.

I learned at a very early age it was all right for my parents to get angry with each other and to demonstrate their rage, but it was not all right for me. I learned that if I had any kind of anger at all, I was to keep it to myself. No wonder I have had such a hard time expressing anger as an adult.

When I was spanked or whipped I was told not to cry. I was told that if I cried I would be whipped harder. And I learned that they meant what they said. As an adult I have had a difficult time feeling it was permissible to show any kind of pain, emotional or physical.

As an alcoholic I learned I could hide my own anger. But I became an expert at provoking others to be angry with me so that I could play the victim role. While you were growing up, I was excellent at remaining calm and pretending that I felt no anger. I became an expert at provoking your mom's anger. It was not until many years later that I was able to recognize the dynamics of my part in initiating many of our arguments. I have felt much remorse as I've looked back on my behavior.

Alcohol allowed me to "numb out." Although there was a part of me that used alcohol so I would not remember certain events, there was another part of me in absolute terror because I was developing more periods of amnesia during my drunken episodes.

The next day after drinking, I can remember so well how frightened I was to know that many hours had gone by and I could not remember a thing that I had done, who I was with, or who I talked with. Yet this did not stop me from drinking again the next night. I believed that alcohol was a magic potion that would help me forget my early fearful boyhood memories. But the alcohol created new fears by wiping out even my most recent memory. I also learned that when we bury our fears so they won't rule our life, what happens is that they rule our life even more. Repressed fears are the ones that really rob us of vitality and happiness. I found myself in a vicious cycle: I drank to get rid of my fear and guilt, making my guilt and fear even stronger, so I continued to drink even more.

Another way that as an adult I have tried to get rid of my fearful little boy was by becoming a workaholic. I think my father was happy to see me living a life where I worked as many hours as I did. I also think he was pleased that I hid my feelings from others as well as myself.

When we are workaholics, there is no time at all to still your mind and go inwards. For years I continued to be a workaholic because I was just too damned scared to go inside. I was afraid that all my fear and guilt would attack me and eat me up.

I learned from my dad that one way of handling anger was to give others the silent treatment. As an adult, I found myself hiding my true feelings from others. If people pressed me for my true feelings, or if I became angry, I would give them the silent treatment. If that didn't work I would resort to pouting like a child. I cringe when I think of what you and Greg learned from me about handling anger.

My fantasy was that being silent was a great way to handle my hostility. I was even more afraid of other people's anger. I thought that if I was silent, my anger would be so camouflaged that no one could get angry at me because I would not be giving out any anger. The irony is that I have come to learn there is nothing more hostile than giving another person the silent treatment. As we both know only too well, many marriages break up because of the lack of honest communication and the husband's hostile use of silence.

Lee, as I think further about my fears I am aware of just how crazy, polarized, and irrational they have been. I have been afraid of closing my eyes or being asleep for fear of what I might miss. I have been afraid of keeping my eyes open for fear of what I might see. I have been afraid to plug my ears for fear of what I might not hear and I have been afraid of listening for fear of what I might hear. I have been afraid of failure, but I have also been fearful of success. The list has gone on incessantly.

I had years of psychoanalysis and other types of therapy, but it was not until I consciously began my spiritual pathway in 1975 that I truly began to heal the injured kid in me. It was my spiritual studies, for me *A Course in Miracles,* that offered me another way of looking at the world and at myself. It showed me the way to forgive others and myself. Twenty years later I am happy to say that I am a far happier person and I continue to have opportunities to heal my fearful child within.

After so many years as an atheist it was strange indeed to begin to live a life where the peace of God became my only goal, forgiveness my only function. I began listening to an inner voice of love, telling me what to think, say, and do.

I finally began to face the pain I had hidden from myself and be willing to look at it differently. Although I had thought I was pretty complete and clean about my father, I have found that there is still more work to be done. And I do believe that as long as I am in this human form, there will always be new temptations to blame, rather than to accept, love, and forgive.

Love,
Dad

The Hidden Little Boy and The Lost Soul

Neither of us ever saw our father's fears of intimacy and love, or his fears about God. So many times in our lives we have been afraid, yet never showed it, sometimes not even to ourselves. We don't feel that we're alone in this. For centuries men have grown up with the firm belief that fathers and other adult men are supposed to be fearless. It is as though this belief had been burned into our male consciousness since we were little children, like a small calf being branded with a branding iron.

We now realize that we were fearful boys who grew up into fathers who had never looked at the fears of the little boy we carried inside. For most of our lives we were not even remotely aware there was a fearful kid that needed our attention and love.

Until a few years ago we did not realize part of the healing we needed to do was with our relationships with our own fathers.

The fearful boy was well hidden. We both appeared on the surface to be self-assured, strong, at times abrupt, controlling, and fast moving. We certainly didn't look fearful from the outside. We now believe what kept us moving so fast was our old fears that had been inside of us since we were little children.

Like us, many men in our culture have lost all awareness of their souls. It has been replaced with the need to achieve, succeed, compete, and conquer. As men, we need to return to our soul. We have found the doorway to this is through our hidden and fearful little boy. The pervasive terror of abandonment that penetrates much of most men's existence has its roots in childhood. Many of us had parents that tried to form us into the child they wanted and the actual child we were was repressed. Eventually we abandoned ourselves and our soul in an attempt to be accepted. How could fear not accompany such a betrayal of self?

From Our Head to Our Heart

In various ways we have attacked each other countless times. Reminding ourselves not to interpret and judge each other's words or behavior has helped greatly in healing our relationship. For example, rather than I (Jerry) labeling Lee as aloof and abrupt at the times I thought he was acting this way, I have found it healing to remind myself that I am actually seeing the symptoms of unrecognized fear. When I (Lee) see my father as not listening but giving advice, instead I discover a different perception of him by choosing to see the fear behind his words rather than reacting to this behavior. We have found that we can open our hearts to each other when we recognize fear, but if we choose to see each other as attacking, we will only attack back.

We found it necessary to work through our anger and resentment with each other. But we also needed to see we were operating out of fear and pain from our childhood. The most healing in our relationship has come from the realization that we both have operated from the same place (fear) while wanting the same thing (love and acceptance). Once we saw this, we could hear each other's fear without so much labeling and judging.

We often found ourselves repeating aspects of our childhood relationship with our father in our adult relationships, both male and female. The process of working through our wounds with our father in other relationships has been a great gift, once *we made it conscious.* Once conscious, we were able to use the relationships in our life for healing. When we kept everything repressed, we usually ended up repeating the same conflicts all over again and creating the same wounds we had with our father.

Symptoms of the Repressed and Fearful Little Boy

We found ourselves walking in grown-up bodies but living in childhood fear. Many men who did not get much in the way of emotional validation and support growing up, spend much of their adult lives trying to prove to themselves and the world that they don't need anything from anybody. Even the term "self-made-man" carries the highest regard in our culture.

As adults we have had long periods where we believed "the man that needs is a man that is weak." So much of our energy was spent with an emphasis on self-sufficiency, we ended up repressing the desire and yearning for connection with God.

Perhaps our biggest defense mechanism was in being incredibly busy in order to keep our fearful little boy quiet and our yearning for God subdued. Like many other men we know, we busied ourselves with endless lists of details and continually over-obligated ourselves. The result was that we overlooked the wholeness of life and the universe.

Why did we do this for so long? Because, like most men, we were afraid. We were afraid of experiencing the wounds of our childhood. We wanted to keep our fearful little boy locked up in a room where nobody would see our pain. But the pain didn't go away; we just masked it. Pain and fear will always find a way to surface. (For a list of common examples of symptoms of the repressed little boy, see Going Further.)

How Fearful Men Show Affection

We believe that until men begin to heal the wounded child and find their soul, their lives will continue to be full of superficial relationships, void of any intimacy. Like many men, for years we yearned for intimacy, yet when we touched it, we became so full of fear that we quickly ran away.

Both of us tried to relate in life the best we could, but for years this meant endless searches of pseudo-affection. Sadly, we each have a history of trying to demonstrate affection through giving money and other material things. Until I (Jerry) began a spiritual path, the words of "emotion" and "love" might as well have been a foreign language. Saying the words "I love you" has not come easy for me (Lee), especially when I am moved to say it to my dad.

It is our impression that most men want their father's love, yet many boys felt more judged and criticized than loved and supported. Though they want love, they also have within them the rebellious adolescent who thumbs his nose at the world. They want to prove they can do just fine without their father's love. Our father–son relationship was a classic example of how we separated from significant people in our lives by creating distance rather than working through our emotions. We were sons that grew up to be men that were good at creating distance, but lousy at expressing affection.

As boys both of us felt as though we were outsiders and didn't really belong anywhere. We frequently felt lost and yearned to be found. We believed our only hope of being accepted was by performing well. We unfortunately had believed what we do is more important than who and what we are.

Even when *what they do* is accepted, many men feel that *who they are* is not. The bottom line is that these men feel unworthy of affection. How can we give in any deep way what we can't accept for ourselves? Consequently most men in our culture feel very uncomfortable giving or receiving affection.

In order to heal our relationships with ourselves and our fathers, we need a willingness to become expressive and authentic human beings. This task has been the most challenging in our lives because it necessitates a willingness to look at our fears and pains. We needed to listen to our hearts rather than our heads before we could see the value of deep and intimate relationships. Most importantly, to heal our relationships there needed to be a willingness to change how we looked at the world. We needed to remember that how much love we give is what life is truly about.

How the Fearful Little Boy is Kept Hidden

We can't heal and nourish our child within as long as we continue behaviors that kept him hidden from us. One of the ways we do this is through fear. As contradictory as it might seem, there is a part of us that wants to keep fear alive. Two of the chief ways we do this is through blame and projection. Both are expressions of fear and together they keep the fearful child in us hidden.

Projection, seeing the cause of our problems as being outside our own minds, keeps us from looking inward at our own pain. When we feel afraid, inadequate, or that we generally don't measure up, there's a part of us that looks for somebody to blame, believing this can relieve our overwhelming inner pain and turmoil. Because we (Lee and Jerry) were ill-equipped to deal with our own internal lives, projection and blame was how we made it through life. Consequently our internal fear was masked. We became very competent individuals, but for years were never really very happy.

From the perspective of our fearful self, projection and blame make perfect sense. "After all," that part of us argues, "we live in an extremely dangerous world. Nobody can be trusted and everybody wants something from us. If you'll just project your inner pain outward, you will become safer." Who doesn't want to feel safe? The problem with this logic is that projection and blame just create more separation and more fear.

It is unfortunate that when sons become fathers, the object of projection often becomes their own sons. We have met many fathers who are gravely disappointed at how frequently they express blame and anger toward their sons, as opposed to love and support. Too often these children grow up feeling they are responsible for their fathers' unhappiness. The son believes that if he were better, brighter, or bigger, then Dad would be happier. It is easy to begin to see the cycle that is built. Without help, these sons will likely grow up to project and blame their own sons, their lovers, and their wives, just as Dad did. It becomes a pattern of behavior that spills over to every family member, regardless of gender.

We each found that in order for us to break the cycle of blame and projection, we had to take responsibility for our healing. This does not mean we should not have anger; it simply means that we need to recognize we are each responsible for our own happiness. We see how we ourselves create and react to our own fear and project it onto others through blame. Once we break that pattern in ourselves, intimacy and self-trust at last become possible.

The irony is that adult fathers and sons commonly get in a Ping-Pong game of blame, tossing the ball back and forth but never picking it up. This never results in joining or healing. Becoming willing to move through anger is often the most difficult of tasks. For years I know that I (Lee) would have felt naked without my anger toward my dad. As long as I blamed him, I did not have to take much responsibility for my own happiness. I think it is precisely this nakedness that we need to be willing to step into.

Allowing Our Children to Help Heal Our Wounds

It is common for men to wound their sons rather than to allow them to heal their wounds. It can feel impossible for a man to join his son in his son's world. We have heard many men say that they could not relate to their sons at all until they were ten or twelve years old. This is because many men are afraid of uncovering their own wounded child within. To join their sons in the child's world feels too dangerous. Of course, none of this is conscious. More likely, the only conscious thought is, "Moms are supposed to take care of the young boys. Men step in to make the sons men." Again there is a denial of the fearful little boy within and a passing on of the hardened, emotionless "man's world."

I (Lee) know that having my children has given me yet another opportunity for healing my childhood pain. My children can be my teachers and my healers, and this can occur at any moment in my entire lifetime. I (Jerry) know that once I saw Lee as my teacher and healer, my guilt was greatly reduced.

To heal our relationship together we only needed to choose the direction of healing.

Let Us Remember

All is interesting to a child's mind,
a spirit fresh and new. What teachers!
Children can help free us from the pain
we carry day in and day out.
Let us join them in their perception,
rather than shutting them down
and bringing our fear and pain to them.
Let us rejoice in their aliveness and make it ours.
Let us remind ourselves of the innocent child within us.
Let us begin to reveal our wounds to our children.
Let our children teach us
that being sensitive and coming from the heart
is what we were born with.
Let us slowly remove our armor
and discover love together.

The Hidden Self

*We heal our minds when we recognize that our thoughts
can be as destructive as our actions.*

One of the fundamental losses that we all have to grieve is that we were raised by imperfect parents in an imperfect society. Our emotional wholeness was taken away from us by the neglect or abuse of our caregivers. We can never fully erase that reality. We can only grieve for it.

MARVIN ALLEN, *IN THE COMPANY OF MEN*

Dear Dad,

While reading the many letters you have sent, I have found myself experiencing a great sense of loss over the man I never knew. I find myself sad, knowing how hidden you kept yourself from others, including your sons. I am sad for you and Greg and me. Sure, we both turned out fine. But as young men we were left on our own to figure out how a man should express his feelings.

In our relationships, I see Greg and myself as both having a tendency to be a lot like you were: overcompliant and inexpressive with what is going on deep inside you. I have never really known what to do with the sea of emotions I experience. When something is bothering me, I process it to death. I'm afraid I would not have made a very good duck, because water does not slide off my back.

I now realize that the many ways you kept yourself hidden weren't your fault. I doubt that you ever thought much about your emotional expressiveness when I was growing up. You were only doing what you had learned as a son.

One thing I have learned is how much of what fathers teach their sons is taught almost unconsciously. I believe that many of the lessons we sons get are "absorbed" rather that learned directly. Even when sons say, "I will never be like him," they take on some of the father's ways. I hear how hidden you were and how much you doubted yourself. I hear how afraid you were of being seen and all the ways you learned to hide. For a long time, I think this is what I covertly learned from you. These were lessons I absorbed and probably are ones you didn't choose for me to get. You have told me at various times about your experiences in medical school. In my own experiences in graduate school I became just like you (perhaps this is why I used to hate to hear the words "you're following in your father's footsteps"). Let me share a little of this with you.

I felt like a failure in high school and I had the bad grades to "justify" my feeling. When I went to college at the University of Oregon I felt as out of place as anyone could feel. I was terrified of anybody getting to know me. For the first time, I found that I wasn't really all that dumb and could get A's if I applied myself. On one hand this was good, but it did not change how I really felt. I immersed myself in my studies to avoid any social contact. My first year of graduate school was so uncomfortable that I dropped out. I was so afraid of being seen, I just left.

In reading your letters, I know you know how this feels. I had become my father's son. I was afraid that if someone saw me, everyone would soon know the truth, that I was a failure and a fraud.

You hid yourself in the haze of alcohol. By the time I was an adolescent, our culture had many more drugs available besides alcohol and I used most of them. Many times I could only let myself be even slightly vulnerable by injecting narcotics, snorting cocaine, or drinking a number of beers. I became my father's son. I used substances to make it through a world I saw as very threatening, and unloving.

As a kid I was angry. I have often wondered where all that anger came from. In reading your letters, I think I have begun for the first time to have some clarity about it.

I remember I wanted you to stand up to Mom more when you would fight. It wasn't that I thought she was wrong about anything, you just seemed so passive. I guess I wanted to see some of your power. You were successful at becoming who you strove to be, which meant you were calm most all of the time. The problem was that you were also distant. In many ways you became your father's son, rarely showing any visible signs of being upset. The only times I did see anger, it was usually directed at me. I have a selective memory about much of this and would like to hear more about how you feel you related emotionally with me.

I wonder if my anger as a kid was your anger. Did I take on a lot of the feelings you were not expressing? Was my rage yours? Was my loneliness, in part, coming from you? Feelings don't just disappear, they remain in the air. Despite you hiding your feelings, I think they leaked out all over the place and I picked them up and made them mine.

As an adolescent, I had a tremendous amount of rage toward Mom and treated her very poorly. Looking back, this has always confused me because I could never really see what she did to cause me to feel that way toward her. I have spent many hours in therapy looking at my relationship with her and where some of this anger came from. It never occurred to me until now that perhaps this anger had very little to do with her. Perhaps I was manifesting your anger.

You are a very fine man and I do not want any of these insights of mine to trigger your guilt. The point is, Dad, you never asked me to take on your anger, just as many other fathers never ask their sons to take on their negative experiences and traits. But sons are like sponges and absorb from their fathers.

If I can see that some of the feelings of anger I have experienced were never mine to begin with, I will be able to more easily release them. This seems like a very important point in my own healing. It also may be helpful for me to hear more about your anger and other feelings. Your ownership may help me release some of the feelings I have carried for you.

There are other ways I have repeated your pattern. As you know, I had more than my share of physical problems as a kid. I faked a lot of illnesses and logged hundreds of hospital days when there was nothing really wrong with me physically, but a lot wrong emotionally. I have shared with you that as a young boy of eight or nine I was in the hospital for some unknown illness (the origin of the illness was me putting the thermometer on a light bulb). You spent a great deal of time in medical libraries trying to find the organic cause. Dad, I was just being like you. You did the same thing, just not with the flare for the dramatic in becoming hospitalized. I faked illnesses to have some semblance of control of what was happening in the family.

Today I am glad to say that I don't feel I have to hide anymore. I do not feel I have any big secrets from you or from anybody else. It feels very good to be able to honestly say that. This doesn't mean I have no problems, but that it's all right for them to be seen. I also think this is true for you. In fact, seeing you change your life was an inspiration for me. It is so important to remember that you didn't teach me just the negative stuff. I also absorbed your willingness to look closely and honestly at your life. I am also my father's son in this regard, and it is a teaching for which I'm most grateful.

Thank you for your willingness to heal our relationship. I am truly fortunate. Seeing all the ways you hid has allowed me to see a lot of things in me that I did not previously recognize.

> In gratitude for who you are,
> Lee

Dear Lee,
You wondered if some of your anger as a child might really have been an expression of my unexpressed anger. I'm sure you are right, although this was not something I would have chosen. As a kid, however, although there were times you

were angry, I think those times were rare. For the most part, you didn't act like an angry child.

My memory is that I was a pretty affectionate father, but that I could turn that off quickly and become strict and demanding. I was not aware that I appeared distant to you, but I must have been. I guess what is important now is that we are both making every effort possible not to be distant, to share our souls with each other. It is not always easy to read what you write, though I know how blessed I am with your willingness to be so vulnerable.

It seems to me, Lee, that each of us in our own life story has become individual experts at selective remembering and selective forgetting. As you and I have talked about our lives together, I have been impressed at how many holes I have in my memory about events and situations that are still quite vivid to you.

On the other hand we have both noticed that you too have holes in your memory about situations where I have a very clear memory. If we can stretch our imaginations, it almost seems we each have half the pieces of a gigantic jig-saw puzzle. As long as we are separate and apart, we can never see the whole picture of the puzzle since each of us has so many holes, or missing pieces. However, when we work together, collecting all our pieces and putting them together, perhaps we'll then stand back one day and see the whole and complete picture.

I have a sneaking suspicion that by the time we finish this book, most of our holes will have disappeared—that we will no longer be struggling with only our half of the pieces.

I used to blame my lack of experiential memory on my dyslexia, but I realize now that my dyslexia only interfered with my rote, sequential memory, like when I try to memo-rize something. I think you were right when you inferred that perhaps I have blamed too many things in my life on my dyslexia.

If I take responsibility for the holes in my memory, then I have to say I have chosen, either consciously or unconsciously, not to remember because it simply was too painful to remember. When memories would be too painful, I would sink them in quicksand so that they would disappear, deep under all the layers of my unconscious. I guess I had some magical thinking that if I buried them deep enough they would no longer bother or threaten me.

Interestingly, I am reminded of the fact that in the 1950s and 1960s I developed expertise in the field of hypnosis. I became an international authority lecturing in different countries. I developed techniques that were helpful in hypnotizing even the most resistant patient. What only a few people know, however, was that I prided myself that no one was able to hypnotize me. Even one of the world's greatest hypnotists, Milton Erickson, was unable to hypnotize me.

I was simply too terrified to let others or myself know what was under the surface. For me, fear played a major role at hiding memories and feelings from my awareness.

I smoked a pipe when I was between the ages of 18 and 50 years old. There are no photos of me during that time when I am not smoking a pipe. As one small example of the strength of my addiction, I remember taking you and Greg, when you were quite young, out on a camping and fishing trip in the Sierras one summer. We rented a boat and rowed a long ways, out to where the fish were supposed to be biting. Then I discovered I did not have my pipe. We immediately rowed back to fetch my pipe from our tent, to your and Greg's dismay and disappointment.

Why was I so addicted to smoking a pipe? My inner secret that I never told anyone was that I smoked a pipe so I could create the impression that I was a very calm and relaxed person. I wanted to appear like a person who never got upset.

I consciously identified with a movie actor of that time by the name of Jean Hersholt. He gave the impression of being a very kind, gentle, and loving man who never got stressed out about anything. I remember one movie where he portrayed a physician. I thought to myself that "I want to be just like him."

In retrospect, I am inclined to think that Jean Hersholt really was this way in life. I don't think that he was even acting. He was naturally a calm, relaxed, and benevolent man.

I was acutely aware that I was not this kind of person and that I had a "tiger by the tail." I was tense, anxious, worried, shy, and had a terrible inferiority complex. By smoking a pipe, I think I wanted to create a picture of a person that was eternally peaceful and calm, all of which I wasn't.

Most of my life, I was play acting and life was a game of pretense. My pipe was my number one prop for acting like the man I wanted to be. I think it is also fair to say that it served the purpose of that little frightened boy inside me, who still wanted to suck his thumb but knew it was not socially acceptable.

Another thing I tried to hide from people was the array of teeth marks where I held the pipe stem in my mouth. Because of my inner tension, I bit down so hard I made holes in the pipe. The pipe industry made a lot of money off me. I had to get new pipes all the time in order to carry out my lie.

I used sickness as a way of getting affection when I was a kid. There was a tremendous amount of secondary gain. I was a pretty sickly kid who was put to bed frequently for a variety of complaints. In looking back, I am sure that many of these illnesses were self-made.

One kind of power I had was that when I was sick my parents stopped fighting. Although I believe I probably felt more powerless than most kids of my day, when I was sick the power was mine. Both of my parents became very caring, soft, and affectionate towards me.

My mom was an amazing, industrious, and creative person. During the year she would save the Sunday comics. At the end of the year she would put all the year's comics together in a big book. She would make a huge book cover for them out of cardboard. The only time my brothers and I could read these comic books was when we were sick. So another secondary gain I had in being ill was to read the giant comic book.

Sometimes being sick backfired on me in every sense of the word. The belief then was that castor oil would make your bowels move and get you well in an instant. As far as I was concerned, the worst tasting medicine ever invented was castor oil. Just smelling it made me want to vomit. My folks would put the castor oil in orange juice, hold my nose, and make me swallow. It more than backfired on me. It was years into my adulthood before I learned to like the taste of orange juice.

Another place where I hid my feelings was inside my muscles. I grew into an adult who had more than his share of stiff necks. This signified to me that life was often a pain in the neck. I also developed a rather rigid and inflexible body. Try as I may, I still can't get my finger tips to touch my toes.

I am convinced that I learned to displace many of my fears, angry feelings, and old pains and sorrows into the muscles of my body. I'm sure that I put a lot of pain, loneliness, and grief into my muscles. I am also convinced that the guilt I carried on my back played a significant role in the chronic back problems I had for so many years.

I, like many other men, learned that it was weak to show your feelings. One of the things I learned to do was to put a fake smile on my face when I was sad. As I mentioned before, I was painfully shy. It always seemed hard for me to meet new people. I remember wanting to avoid their eyes. I was afraid that if they looked into my eyes they might see the real me and they would not like what they saw.

I tried to be a "pleaser" and would do anything and everything to please people. I always wanted everybody's approval. I did not have the slightest clue how to say no to anybody. I did everything to hide my bad grades in school and all my feelings of failure and inadequacy.

Even after medical school these symptoms were still prominent. For obvious reasons I have always dreaded examinations because that is where it is hardest to hide how dumb and stupid you really are.

For example, I was taking my boards in psychiatry and neurology—three days of grueling testing. I studied faithfully and diligently for the exams. But at exam time I wanted to hide my feelings of fear. I put so much energy into acting "cool as a cucumber." Just about everyone remarked about how relaxed I looked. I worked so hard on my disguise that I flunked the exams.

Six months later I took the exams again. This time I let more people know how scared I was and I exerted no effort at hiding my feelings—including how many times I had to go to the bathroom before the exam. But then the miracle happened—I passed the exam. It was a pretty good lesson for me on the value of being real. Yet shortly after the exam I was back to hiding my feelings once again. It would take many years before I could more consistently let myself be seen.

As a child I seemed to pick up the wrong learning cues. I became convinced that if you let people come too close to you, you would get hurt. So I became an expert at building imaginary fences around my heart. It started with my dad and mom and then went out to everyone else.

I remember my fence routine in high school. I bragged that I wanted to play the field and would not date the same girl more than three times. The true reason was that I did not want to let a girlfriend get close to me. I was afraid the fence would come down and I would get hurt again.

There used to be a television program called "To Tell The Truth." On the show there would be three people in chairs. They would tell a story and answer questions depicting what one person had done and something about their personality. The contestants were supposed to guess which was the real person. They would then play some music and the real person would stand up and everyone would applaud.

For so much of my life, Lee, I have been so confused about who I really was because I tried to pretend to be so many people other than myself. If someone had asked for the "real Jerry" to stand up, I would not have known which of those many people inside me was real. I would have stayed stuck in my seat.

It has always been difficult for me to define the empty place inside me. It is almost as if there are not words to adequately define it. Perhaps it is more of a nonverbal experience. At any rate, I have just re-read the above and am in touch again with the hole within myself. For so long, I have felt separate and lonely and cried out inside for help. I am thankful that I can now share this with you.

Love,
Dad

Finding Ourselves Through Knowing Our Fathers

Until we developed the willingness to be expressive with our feelings, we remained outside life. For years we were endlessly imprisoned in self-imposed solitary confinement, walking around half-dead. Until we recognized the fundamental importance of knowing our fathers and our children, we continued to feel lost and without direction.

Robert Bly suggests that unless we discover and embrace our father's feelings of rejection and grief, we can't heal our own feelings of rejection and grief. For us, this is an important point. *We begin to heal ourselves by coming to know our fathers.*

Like us, many sons have been in some way emotionally shut down by their fathers or their fathers were missing from the very beginning. We grew up not knowing how to express all our feelings, or how to even appreciate the value of this ability. In becoming more feeling and expressive men, it was helpful to take a look at who our fathers were and what their childhoods were like. We found that just the simple act of getting an idea of what our father's life was like was very healing. (For an exercise in finding your father, see Going Further.)

Doing Versus Being

In our culture a man's worth is often determined by what he does rather than by who he is. At various times, both of us (Lee and Jerry) have fallen into this belief. We each reached adulthood with the firm belief that our value to other men, women, our families, and society was directly linked to our ability to perform, achieve, and provide. For years, we saw anything that got in the way of these abilities as a threat. And we saw any type of inner, spiritual search as a threat and something to be avoided.

When we talked to each other and other men, we were much more comfortable talking about what we were doing than what we were feeling. Our conversations were usually devoid of any depth, reporting only what we were accomplishing, what we had done in the past, or what we were planning to do in the future. Until we consciously chose otherwise, we lived a life of judgment, comparison, and competition, with little or no true sense of self.

It is time that men not only allow themselves to become more expressive in who they are, but also give reflective thought to what they do. It is too common for a man to work until 65, retire, and die a few years later without truly knowing himself. It is as though these men choose death over the uncomfortable ambiguity of asking the question, "Who am I?"

The Body and the Experience of Feelings

Both of us have a history of ignoring our body and the experience of feelings in order to achieve, win, compete, and succeed. In different ways, each of us has become more aware of our body, and as a result, found ourselves able to experience greater depth in feeling. Like us, many men further shut off experiencing their feelings by shutting off from their bodies. Men treat their bodies like machines that their heads and hearts ride around on. Like a person who drives a car that badly needs service because they have to get there, many men ignore their bodies in order to do what their egos say is important.

Illness can be a defense against experiencing our feelings. Both of us (Lee and Jerry) have a history of back pain. We have found that most often our suppressed feelings have an influence on our back problems. Sadly, we are not alone. Thousands of men die each year from illnesses directly related to the suppression of feelings. In our own lives we have come to firmly believe that:

1. Our beliefs and attitudes affect our health.
2. The ability to express in healthy ways what we are feeling is vital to our emotional and physical health.

Men primarily learn about attitude and the expression of feelings from their fathers or other men. If most men are suppressing the expression of feeling, then we are passing on a lineage that quite realistically can kill our sons.

The good news is that our illnesses can become wake-up calls, alerting us to start looking at and experiencing our inner lives. For us, reading books about men, seeking help with our relationships, adopting a body awareness practice (yoga, martial arts, dance, and others), and spending more time with men in honest, sharing environments, have assisted us in healing.

We have found the following to be truths about our bodies and our feelings:

- When we hold angry feelings inside and don't express them, our bodies are negatively affected. This is true even if we deny our anger.

- There is no such thing as hiding our feelings from our bodies. Our bodies react to both our conscious and unconscious thoughts.

- When we hold onto unforgiving thoughts and feelings, we are prone to attacking our bodies.

- There is no such thing as a neutral thought. We can take charge of our emotional and physical health by taking charge of our thoughts and beliefs.

- Listening to our bodies can be the doorway to our freedom. Our bodies can be windows into what we are not seeing inside of us.

- It is not people or situations outside ourselves that cause conflict. Our own thoughts and attitudes cause us distress. Thoughts affect both our emotions and our bodies.

- Health is inner peace. We lack any semblance of inner peace when we keep our true feelings and fears hidden from ourselves and those close to us.

The Desire to Belong

There is one thing that we have always felt but often denied as men—the desire to connect with other men (especially our fathers and sons) and feel part of the community of men. Until we (Lee and Jerry) really examined our lives and our purpose, our daily lives were an array of separated and isolated tasks. We often found ourselves feeling alone and alienated, yearning for more connectedness.

In our culture, men have become disenfranchised from feelings and male connection. We have compartmentalized our feelings to such a degree that we are afraid to share our feelings and vulnerability with both men and women. The hunger for connection with our fathers and sons goes deeper than what most men experience at a conscious level. For us, it has been a remarkable experience to say to each other "You are important to me and I want to know you. I want to try to find some way to connect with you, even though I don't know if it is possible."

Wounding Others

Everything presented in this section is equally applicable to all of our relationships. They are magnified with father and son.

We have found in our father–son relationship that projection is one of the most common defense mechanisms there is for handling our pain. Rather than experiencing and expressing our feelings, both of us have turned to projecting our pain and guilt onto each other, and have then attacked.

These projections have an unconscious mechanism that was part of our denial that we were in any pain or had any guilt. After we denied our feelings, we projected them onto others just like a motion picture projector projects an image on a movie screen. We each habitually projected the pain from our inner guilt onto someone else—often each other.

There were times when we would attack each other and feel satisfaction, control, and even righteousness. We almost succeeded in convincing ourselves that the other person was always the cause of our pain. We blamed each other and at times withdrew our support and affection. For me (Lee), my dad received a great deal of my anger and I walked around in life feeling like a victim who had been unjustly treated. In this situation, peace was impossible.

The lesson presented to us over and over again is that we have great temptations to project onto other people the very feelings we don't want to admit that we have inside ourselves. In the past when I (Jerry) felt guilty, I have often tried to make other people feel guilty; many times this was my son, Lee. When I (Lee) have been hurt and wounded, I have often tried to blame and wound my dad. The common thread of projection is we do not want to own our inner experience and feelings.

It has been helpful for us to recognize that *"I am never upset for the reason I think."* (A Course in Miracles, second edition, Workbook Lesson 5, page 8)

To begin healing this process, we became aware that whenever we were blaming each other or were intensely angry, we were very likely projecting. At these times it was helpful to ask ourselves, "What is really underneath what we are feeling?" Usually, this makes us take a second look and often we get in touch with the feelings inside us. And we begin to be able to get closer to the roots of the issue that's bothering us. We are certainly not perfect at it, but we now find ourselves more willing to pause and look within when we are tempted to fall into blaming or attacking each other. This has not been easy to do and the following is a rough idea of what helped us with our communication.

1. We are willing to realize that we both probably want the same things: to be heard, loved, and accepted. We also realize we both have things we don't want: to be interrupted, attacked, or judged.

2. We recognize one truth in our communication: We will likely get back whatever we put out. If we are feeling we want to attack, we will likely anticipate and experience being attacked. If we own our experiences and communicate with love, we will experience peace of mind. This does not mean we should not express anger when we feel it. It does mean looking at how we can communicate all feelings while maintaining our inner focus of love.

When we are tempted to talk to each other about another person, we resist the temptation and talk about us. We have found that the best way to do this is to begin to communicate with "I" statements rather than "you" statements. Rather than saying "Dad, you never should have done that. What kind of father would do a thing like that," we would say, "I feel scared when you do that. I am angry, but I am not sure exactly what is going on in myself. I would like to talk to you about it." When we are making "you" statements, it is likely that we are projecting. When making "I" statements, it is likely that we are taking responsibility for our feelings and communicating, healing, and joining.

The Fence Between Father and Son

One thing that as a father and son we know to be true: we deeply want to be close, to share from the heart, in an intimate way. Through the years, we developed a fear of these very things. We became afraid of closeness with each other. We built emotional fences between us in an effort to overcome these fears.

When we are truly honest with ourselves, we see that in part, we built fences because each of us feared the other's power. We came to realize that we really feared our own power. As is the case in many dynamics of the father and son relationship, we found parallels on the spiritual level. In many instances in this section the word "father" can be replaced with the word God or higher power. We fear the power of God so we build a fence separating ourselves from God. Yet often it is the power of God within us that we fear.

Many times in the process of trying to show caring, we built a fence instead. For example, I (Jerry) sometimes communicated by being critical and by giving advice because I wanted Lee to do well. But what occurred was that I (Lee) became afraid of talking with Dad because I was fearful he would not approve, or he would question me instead of just listening.

I (Jerry) did not really know how to be a friend to Lee while being a father. Like many fathers, I would go from one extreme to another, but unfortunately I was not very successful at marrying friendship and fatherhood. We have both realized that as fathers we have the difficult task of joining our children in friendship while at the same time modeling manhood.

I (Lee) wanted nothing more than to have a close relationship with my dad. But I came to realize during adolescence that although I could push my dad away, my attempts at bringing him closer constantly failed. Like many sons, I became an expert at provoking anger in my father but usually felt helpless at creating an atmosphere where it was safe to express or receive love. I did not know how to take the fence down, but I sure knew how to build them!

The process of writing this book has reinforced our belief that finding ourselves involves sharing ourselves. In closing this chapter we invite you to read the following poem.

I'll Meet You Beyond the Fences

As I wake on this new day,
may the depth of my being reveal itself to me
in the fresh, innocent, drinkable light of dawn.

May all of who I am be shown to myself
and to whom I love,
with no shame,
with no guilt.
May I find the joy of being known
cleanse my soul and spur me on in my life.
Today I reclaim my aliveness
and I choose to share it with all I meet.

No longer need I be afraid of my feelings and love.
My inner life is the doorway to being more fully alive.
Experiencing and expressing my feelings
is natural, important, and valuable.

SEVEN

What Fathers Teach Their Sons About Women

If we truly believe in equality between men and women,
it will be demonstrated in every part of our lives.

What we seek appears to be an entirely new kind of relationship between women and men. A quest for a true equality must be based upon a deeper understanding and a new respect for our differences. It seems that at this juncture in human evolution, it is more useful to embrace religious and philosophical belief systems that honor the sacredness and inherent value of both sexes.

AARON KIPNIS & ELIZABETH HERRON,
WHAT WOMEN AND MEN REALLY WANT

Dear Dad,

Before writing this book, I never gave much thought to what you taught me about relating to women. I've done a lot of reflection about your relationship with Mom and your divorce, but somehow I never took the next step and looked at the way you related to women and the way that influenced my relationships with women.

I have kept a journal of feelings and memories that came up as I read and talked to others about men's relationships with women. I have been amazed at what has emerged and would like to share this with you. We have not talked about this subject before and what I present is my experience. It may have little to do with what was actually going on with you, but if you would like to clarify or expand on any of these areas, I would welcome it.

I saw you as a man who, underneath it all, had respect for all life. I saw you as a person who was popular and well respected by others. Yet I also saw you as a man who never felt very comfortable around others and who may have felt like he never really belonged. For years this all became true for me, especially with women. I think I have moved more and more toward letting myself be known by others without feeling guarded or ashamed, but I must admit I still often feel a sense of being just a little on the outside. You taught me a deep respect for other life, yet you also taught me about being isolated, lonely, and self-conscious. As I have said in other letters, in the past I tried to deal with these feelings in the same ways you did: through overwork, overachievement, and substance abuse.

•

I never saw you having all that much fun in life. Other than at cocktail parties, I don't remember seeing you and Mom laugh very often. I never heard you complain much, but I think I got an overall picture that a man's job in relation to a woman includes three things: work, work, and work.

This is all new in my mind, but I think that I learned that a man gets validation from a woman through being an achiever. I saw that Mom was proud of your achievements, but I also saw her devalue you in your arguments together. I learned from this that the best insulation from being inadequate in a woman's eyes is to work hard and suffer. I think if you had been freer, more joyful, less hard working, more spontaneous, you would not have gotten as much praise. In fact, in our family, praise was given more for suffering than for enjoying life. The comment, "I worked until midnight, boy am I tired," would be met with more positive reinforcement than, "I left work early and went fishing, boy am I relaxed."

In my second marriage, I found myself becoming dull and predictable. Before being married there seemed to be a freedom in being romantic, spontaneous, and joyful. After having kids, I fell into the "work hard and suffer" mode. Unconsciously, I believed this would gain me praise from my wife and would insulate me from any criticism. I think that, in part, Carny began to see me as kind of boring and not very much fun. This confused the hell out of me because I thought unconsciously that I was doing what I was supposed to do in relation to her: work hard and suffer.

More recently, I have begun to realize some of this, and have decided for myself to enjoy life and do more of what I want to do. This does not mean that I ignore my responsibilities; it actually means that I embrace *all* of them, including having joy. In this capacity, I let my children be my teacher.

•

Even though you were a psychiatrist, I did not find you to be a very good listener. With Mom I saw you usually in one of two modes: You were either being quiet and tolerant or you were interrupting and directive. Though I am sure these were not the only ways you and Mom communicated, they are the ones that stood out for me and that I adopted in relation to women.

Despite being a good listener in my office and with my kids, I have really had to work at being even a moderately good listener with my wife. For a long time in our personal couple's work, I found myself not really able to listen to Carny with great depth. I wanted to, but I kept expecting her to say painful things. Much of my energy went toward trying to tolerate my anxiety and what was being said. When I couldn't tolerate anymore, I would interrupt. Sometimes, once my lips started to move, they would not stop. I do think I've made significant progress toward becoming a good listener, but I still have to fight my old pattern of interrupting.

I must say that I see you relating to women today in a totally different way. You are much more able to listen and communicate what is happening inside you and I rarely see you interrupt.

Your method of expressing caring followed from your role as listener and interrupter. To show caring, I saw you give advice. Essentially I perceived you as a problem solver. I am not totally sure, but I think this was more pronounced with women.

I think this is a very common experience for men. We listen for the problem so we can then go about solving it. It is a form of caring. Unfortunately, with Mom, I do not think she ever really felt heard by you.

My guess is that many of your arguments with Mom were the result of different styles of communicating. You wanted to show that you cared by solving problems and moving on to the next thing. Mom wanted you to listen and validate what she was saying, without needing to solve the problem right away. I know that I am making some guesses here as to what was going on for each of you, but it is what I took away. There was not right or wrong, just different ways of communicating.

Out in the world, you seemed so different than you were back home. I don't know what went on when you were not in front of us kids, but I didn't see you as being very strong with Mom. This is not to say that I always wanted you to be dominant, but Mom did seem to be the boss. I know this is how Grandpa was and maybe you were doing the only thing you knew how.

In contrast, I saw you very strong and dedicated in your work. My feeling was that nobody told you what to do and that if they did, you would not have stood for it.

I find it difficult to say "no" to Carny. It's not that she always expects me to say "yes," just as Mom probably didn't with you, but I feel almost obliged to make her happy. I think I have some fear, as I believe you did, that if I am firm with my boundaries, I will end up alone.

I think we are not the only ones caught in this dynamic. Many men fear their own strength and fear rejection. This makes us "yes" men with women. This ultimately robs us of both personal power and intimacy with our partners.

I am not sure what I learned from you about sexuality and relating to women. As I have mentioned before, I don't remember any real conversations except for one time, and all I remember is you asking me if I had wet dreams yet.

I had my first sexual experience at age 13. I look at 13-year-old kids today and I just can't imagine them having sex, though unfortunately I know many are. I had no idea what to do. The whole thing was disastrous. It happened during a party at our house and the girl was drunk. She was a little older than me. In the middle of the whole thing she threw up on me. I was off to a rather confusing sexual start.

I had my first serious girlfriend when I was a sophomore in high school. Lorna was a very sweet and beautiful girl, with a heart of gold. I wanted so much to be kind to her, yet I found myself treating her like a second-class citizen. I remember not wanting to do this, yet it was as if it was automatic. I think it illustrated just how confused about relationships with women I was, and how much your and Mom's relationship affected me. I wanted to treat her like the fine person she was, yet frankly I often treated her like an object with no feelings.

I believe you felt there were constant demands coming from Mom. I do not know if there were, but the impression I got was that you felt women were always demanding. Looking at your mom it is not hard to see where this originated.

I think that I learned this belief from you and it has taken some doing to shed it. For years, I was always a little on guard with women because I believed there would be demands placed upon me and it would be my obligation to meet them, no matter what they were (my guess is that you also believed the same for years). Believing these two things made it difficult to just relax in a relationship.

In relation to this, I never saw you express dissatisfaction. The only time I knew you were dissatisfied was when you told me you and Mom were getting a divorce. Looking back,

I can see that you were not really happy, but back then I didn't know. I think you taught me that expressing dissatisfaction to a woman is not something that men do. Men are supposed to take it until they can't take it anymore, then they leave.

The main ways I saw you relate to Mom was by reporting how your day was or what you were going to do the next day. I did not see much communication of feelings. I do not see this as unusual among fathers and it may be a common occurrence. I learned from you that feelings are to be relegated to the hidden, inner world of men and communication with women should be a series of reporting events.

As I write this, I wonder if you and Mom related differently in private. I don't know. I do know that I do not have many memories of you talking about your inner feelings. As I recall, conversations with you usually consisted of you trying to elicit reports from others, sometimes relating a report of something you were doing, but rarely about anyone's inner process.

Curiously, I have fallen to the other extreme in my relationship. I find myself wanting to process almost everything to the point that sometimes just an everyday, casual conversation is difficult with me. This is probably where all of my training and personal therapy can be a hindrance. It's not unusual for Carny to say, "Why does everything with you have to be so heavy?" And she is right. I do need to lighten up a lot of the time.

Dad, there were times I saw you treat many women rudely, abruptly, and sometimes with a mean streak. Mostly these women were in vocational positions that you may have seen as lower than yours. I would often hear you being very short and discourteous to your answering service (back then, mostly women). My guess is that, like many men, you felt controlled by the women in your life (Mom and Grandma). Women "beneath you" became easy targets for your anger and frustration.

Though I do not follow your exact pattern, I have regrettably found myself being more intimidating and controlling with women than I would like to be. Though I have changed since my first girlfriend, there are times when I am not very understanding and I find myself adopting an attitude of superiority. This is the opposite of what I believe. I believe in and want equality in relationships with women, but sometimes the thread of superiority and righteousness won't go away. I am working on reducing this by being honest with women whenever these feelings arise. When I do this, I am always moved by how it deepens my relationships.

As I have thought about the patterns that I fall into, I have seen they are often a mirror image of how I saw you relating to Mom. I want to emphasize that I realize your experience may be quite different than mine. I also want to acknowledge that we both have grown in how we relate to women.

For years I fell into three patterns with women when it came to conflict, and I think these came from how I experienced you.

You seemed to be pretty good at *avoiding* conflict in general. Not being around was one way you did this. Alcohol was also a good way. I certainly did this; starting at a very early age, I avoided conflicts in relationships by using drugs.

Sometimes, when you were backed into a corner, you seemed to *confront* what was happening. On the heels of this, I would see you finally *comply* with Mom's wishes. I saw you

like a toothless tiger, occasionally roaring, but always back-
ing down. In past relationships, I fell into this pattern too.

Dad, in closing this letter I would like to acknowledge
that both of us have improved in our ability to enjoy intimacy with women. I really admire the relationship that you
have with Diane, and I know it did not just happen but took
a lot of personal work on your part. I look forward to more
conversations with you about the contents of this letter.

I also want to acknowledge that you taught me respect,
compassion, and love for humanity in general. This has served
me well.

In peace,
Lee

Dear Lee,
On first reading your letter, I had to ask myself, "Do I really
want some of the things you said about our family experiences to be made public? Is it really okay for others to read
this and know how crazy I really was during those days?"
The answer is yes, it is okay, but I have to admit that my first
reaction was embarrassment.

Frankly, I found myself of two minds reading your letter.
I was most happy that you could share your perceptions of
those earlier experiences with me. I had a fleeting fantasy of
wishing that you had chosen to identify with my strengths
rather than my weaknesses. Again, our memories are different. I remember more than just a few times that we talked
about relationships with women and sex, memories that you
do not seem to recall.

In regard to problems in my marriage with your mother,
they had been out in the open for a long time. Some of our
perceptions about what led up to the divorce remain pretty
different. There were two long separations before the final

separation that led to the divorce. It was my decision to leave. I thought the friction and fights were too much for me to bear any longer. I remember that you were upset about the divorce, but not surprised.

Now to recollect what I learned from my dad about women: When I think about what my dad taught me about women, I find myself first putting a high-powered microscope solely on the negative things. In order to give a more accurate picture, I need to remind you myself, once again, that during my father's day the most important thing a father could do was provide for his family.

My father worked his heart out to provide, always trying to make sure that his kids had educational and other advantages that he never had. It was a time of survival without the luxury of contemplative time.

My dad and mom had one of those relationships where they couldn't live with or without each other. They cared for each other in many ways. Yet, in their own way, I believe they cared for and loved each other.

I was very fortunate to have had parents who cared so dearly for their sons and did absolutely their very best to be good parents. Their models for parenting and loving were their own parents. If I had received the same parenting as they did, I am certain I would have behaved the same way my parents did.

It is my belief that, in some way I don't quite understand, we choose our parents. I think all the positive and negative lessons I learned from my parents were lessons I needed to learn in this lifetime.

As I grew older, I began to realize what a strong woman my mother was and that the power of our immediate family was with her. My impression was that she was firm and strong in her opinions, and everyone respected and obeyed her wishes. They would not have dared otherwise. She had the makings of a matriarch. However, as powerful as she was, it was my grandmother who was really the head of the clan.

I had many uncles and aunts living in Southern California. Once a year, all the family, aunts and uncles and cousins, would have a family pot luck picnic at Bixby Park in Long Beach, California. There was always enough food to feed an army and a wonderful time was had by all.

When my maternal grandmother died, it was as if we had lost our leader. Everyone missed her desperately. From my viewpoint, after she died no one seemed to be there to take on the leadership. Though my mother reigned in our family, she never took up the role my grandmother had held. One of the first things I sadly noticed was there were no more annual family picnics.

I don't know much about my dad's father, but I would bet that my grandma ran the show there. As I grew up and began to look at my aunts and uncles, I would say, and again I emphasize this is only my impression, that for the most part the women acted like the "boss" of the family in almost all areas of decision making.

As I grew older and put on my psychiatric "hat," I had the distinct impression that my dad and uncles tended to marry women who were like their mothers, and they very closely identified with their fathers by taking a subservient role in the family.

My dad could do a very energetic and exciting dance from his native Russia, the *korobushka*. When I watched my dad do this dance, holding his hands to the floor behind him, kicking his legs straight up in the air, it was like he was another man. I did not know that he had that much energy in him, or that much joy.

I do remember conversations at family gatherings where

my aunts would make it sound like their husbands were the strong ones and the decision makers. I think perhaps some of the husbands thought they were. But from my viewpoint, my aunts were only feeding their husband's illusions.

I had a friend named James living across the alley. His father was a huge man. There was no question that James's father made all the decisions in their family. He was a most demanding man, always shouting at his children and his wife. James told me that his dad drank a lot.

I remember he used to beat the living daylights out of James for the most minor infractions. I was scared of that man and didn't like being around him. There were many times that James's mother would have bruises on her face and arms. James's mother used to tell me and others that she was clumsy and fell down a lot. I was gullible enough then to believe her. Little did I realize what kind of physical abuse was going on right next door to me!

So what did I learn from the father next door? I learned some men felt they could control their world by making everyone afraid of them. I learned there were some men who felt it was okay to unmercifully abuse their wives, physically and emotionally

In those days, many women seemed to accept the role of being second-class citizens and acted as if they inherited the victim role because of their gender. It was a time when very few women dared to think freely and independently.

I don't remember my dad sitting me down and having a conversation about women. We never talked about sex. That was just not in him to do and was not his style of communication. So I learned from Dad by direct observation or by hearing his remarks when he was upset and at his wit's end with my mom.

I learned from my dad that women were to be feared and

not to be trusted. I learned that women were the enemy. If you get too close to them, you will get hurt.

Out of fear, my dad used deception with my mom. For example, my older brother Les decided to go to Switzerland to study and obtain a Ph.D. in chemistry. My mom was furious with him for going to Europe to study and refused to send him money.

Every month I saw my dad taking money from the cash register and sending it to my brother. He hoped my mom would never find out. As far as I know, she never did.

I remember my dad trying to get my sympathy and support. He pouted a great deal. He would moan and groan with me and ask what had he done in his life that God would want to punish him by having him live with such a witch. I guess I learned from my dad that God used women to punish men.

There were times that Dad encouraged me to be a peace maker. I remember trying to play that role, always unsuccessfully. More frequently than not, I would end up becoming the enemy of them both.

I learned from my dad that it is possible to give up your fatherly role to your wife. In many ways, it seemed that my mom took on the role that most fathers played during the time I was trying to grow up.

I also learned from my dad that it is possible to abdicate for periods of time your father and husband role and revert to the role of a child. It is possible to let your wife treat you like a child, to hate her for doing that, to love her for doing that, and to hate yourself for putting yourself in this role. I learned that it is possible to go out and find a woman who will mother you, so you can feel you are at long last getting the mothering you felt you never received.

I learned from my dad that it is possible to feel so inadequate and guilty about making the wrong decision, it is safer to give that decision making to a woman and give your power away. If you are not making decisions, you don't have to take responsibility for them. And as you know Lee, for much of my life I had tremendous problems making any kind of decision.

My mom could be extremely volatile and unpredictable. My parents could be kind and apparently loving to each other—then one wrong word from my dad could cause an explosion of the worse sort. Unfortunately, I learned it is a very risky proposition to be intimate with women. I learned to never relax when you are feeling close to a women because the next moment a bomb might go off.

Although for a long time I identified with my father about family conflicts, as time went on it became clear he played an equal role in creating them. In retrospect, I can see that the cause was not one person. It was a dance they did together.

There were many times I asked my dad why he did not divorce my mother. He never answered my questions. I think he believed a commitment was a commitment. He believed when you were married, there always had to be a way to work out the relationship.

Perhaps it was my dad's relationship with God that kept my mom and him together. I always felt my dad had a very close connection with God, although he rarely talked about it. I always felt it was his trust and faith in God that gave him the strength to cope with circumstances that were frequently so adverse. Somehow, although he was frequently very pessimistic and not always connected with God, there was another part of him that always held onto hope for his marriage. I do believe this was one of Dad's greatest strengths. It took me decades to learn that lesson from him.

Lee, I have just reread what I have written; once again, old pangs of guilt have arisen. I experience a deep sadness that somehow I chose to recycle some of the old conflicts with my parents upon you and Greg. I wanted so much to be a different kind of father for you. This is not to take away all the positive things I know happened between us.

I have spent an enormous amount of time releasing all the guilt I had from not fulfilling either of our expectations of what a loving father might be. I have even written books on it, such as *Good Bye to Guilt*. Just when I am beginning to realize that there is no value in guilt, I find some of that old guilt popping up again. I find there is more inner work to be done.

For me, my life-long healing process feels like peeling an onion that does not seem to get smaller. There are layers beneath layers. In writing this letter, it feels like tears coming up from a sadness I didn't think existed anymore.

> Love,
> Dad

How Men's Beliefs About Women are Developed

One way of looking at children is to imagine their minds and hearts are made of very impressionable, delicate, and sensitive photographic film that make a three-dimensional color imprint of everything they experience. Thousands of heart prints and mind prints are made each day. Every child's personality and future male–female relationships are shaped by their parents. When we look back at our childhood, we realize that we paid very close attention to our father's actions. Like most children, we were highly aware when words and actions were not in harmony with each other.

Like most men, we have repeatedly heard the statement, "you can't live with 'em, you can't live without 'em," when men were talking about women. It reflects a pervasive belief that women are needed for our happiness, yet will lead us to despair. What a double-bind to be holding in our consciousness!

We have found the key to healing this double-bind lies in being able to see that connection and independence are not opposites at all, but in fact complement one another. We believe that a successful and happy marriage occurs when both parties are supported and encouraged in their independence while maintaining an intimate connection.

Lie to Get What You Want

At times, both of us saw our fathers treating women—our mothers in particular—as if they needed to be controlled, manipulated, feared, and avoided.

We both recall times when our fathers were either blatantly dishonest or very secretive with our mothers. In talking with other men, we have found this is not unusual. Why do some men, even ones we think are honest, lie or keep secrets from their spouses? Perhaps they feel they are always about to get into trouble. Many men adopt the same technique for avoiding "punishment" as they did with their mothers: be secretive or lie.

Women Don't Trust Men

As adolescents, we got sexually aroused but did not know how to deal with our desires. Neither of our fathers talked about this. When we were in high school and college, most males would say anything to get a woman into bed. Sex is one obvious area where men lie to women. Movies show it as permissible, if not manly, to lie to get a woman into bed, then lie again to get her out of the house the next day.

Trust has been a very real problem for both men and women.

This is complicated by the pervasive belief among men that women cannot be trusted, and among women that men cannot be trusted. Neither of us saw our parents as always demonstrating trust and integrity.

Today it is common to see inconsistent integrity among men in the political arena. Even when endorsing a certain candidate, people state they do not fully trust them. President Ronald Reagan had the nickname "Teflon Ron," suggesting that he could slide out of any situation by lying. President Bill Clinton had the nickname "Slick Willy," suggesting he does not always tell the truth. What is important here is not just that we don't trust politicians are honest, but that culturally we have come to distrust any man in authority. We have to wonder if perhaps we have created this through our projections from our distrustful fathers.

Like us, most men learn from their fathers through what Deborah Tannen calls "report" talk. Most women's messages are sent via "rapport" talk. In rapport talk, women connect with one another on a personal level by *establishing relationships*. In report talk, men talk to *maintain status* in a hierarchical order.

For years, we (Lee and Jerry) communicated as most men do: in negotiating, pragmatic, independence-preserving ways. We did this because we saw our fathers and other men doing the same. It was the manly thing to do. For years what women wanted—intimacy and emotional contact—felt threatening to us. We feared for the rejected little boy within and we guarded ourselves constantly against and loss of our status.

We discovered that when we communicated solely by report talk, trust is seldom established. It was important for us to see that there is nothing inherently dishonest in us or other men, only that we simply do not always have the skills to talk on a more feeling level and connect on a personal level with other men and women.

Don't Listen, Just Fix It

When we were growing up, neither one of us would have described our fathers as good listeners. Unfortunately we have found most adult sons have had a similar experience. When we ask adult sons how often they saw their fathers actively and supportively listening to their mothers, we are met with either chuckles or looks of confusion. It is as though we asked how many fathers were on the first flight to the moon.

It is certainly not new information that when a woman is speaking about a concern or personal problem, generally she wants to be heard and supported. And what's becoming clear is that most men want that, too! Despite this knowledge, both of us have had our share of difficulties with women in relationships because of our belief that when somebody is talking about a problem, it is our job to "fix" it.

We grew up to believe that conversation nearly always present challenges to be met and problems to be solved. As long as we limited ourselves to that set of beliefs we tended to feel inferior if we were not solving problems. We are sure that both of us being in the helping professions is no accident since it is here that we can legitimately have this kind of relationship with the people we serve. Even here, however, the trend is away from "fixing" and more toward truly listening to people and guiding them to discover and embrace their own greatest strengths.

For years, we both thought it was our task to find a set of solutions to problems. This was even more true if the person talking to us was a woman about whom we cared deeply. Unfortunately, the result was often that these women felt unheard by us, even when we were doing our very best to show we cared by trying to solve the problem.

In talking with my dad, I (Lee) have discovered one reason why he was gone so much of the time. When he felt he was failing at being a good problem solver at home, he would disappear rather than continue to feel ashamed and incompetent. He became involved in activities where he could feel competent; for him, it was work. For other dads it may be golf, fixing the car, or working in the yard. The healing part for me is to see that he really did care. Much of his absence, be it physical or in alcohol, was coming from a place in him where he felt incompetent. My heart opened to him as I realized this. It also helped me to recognize when I am tempted to do the same.

Finding solutions to problems is a wonderful skill to have. But if it is the only skill, true listening becomes quite difficult. We found it very useful to begin balancing our problem solving skills with sincere and loving listening skills. When we are actively listening, we do not interrupt, and we do not ask a lot of questions as if we were playing "twenty questions." Instead we listen, state to the person what we heard them say, and honor their feelings even if we do not understand or agree with what they are experiencing. We listen with the heart rather than trying to solve a problem with our intellect.

Women are Dangerous

As you can see from my letters, I (Jerry) came from a home where my father was dominated and controlled by my mother. I (Lee) feel that my dad adopted many of my grandfather's ways. As boys, we both had times when we perceived our fathers as weak. We both had to work on not seeing women as dangerous beings or out to steal our masculinity. There was a part of our unconscious—a very dark past—that wanted to believe women are largely destructive, not to be trusted, and always ready to take our power away at any moment.

It is important to note that this did not come from our mothers. Our unconscious creates images by watching the dynamics between our parents. In particular, sons watch how their fathers react toward the women in their lives and create illusions that are seldom accurate. What we internalize is often not even close to how someone really is.

No man wants to be helpless, totally reliant on another, endlessly needy, and essentially weak. We realized if we believed a relationship with a woman would ultimately result in this, we would certainly see women as the enemy. What is healing to know, however, is that we only needed to let go of our fears to find our own strength and open our eyes to a very different view of women. The fears that held us back have had far more to do with what we picked up from our fathers' than our mothers' true identities. To understand this has been truly liberating.

Psychological and Physical Abuse

There are many ways that men use women as scapegoats, ranging from constant verbal criticism to physical abuse. Regardless of the form, this underlying belief is passed onto the son: Women are to blame; use them as scapegoats. Let us look at what happens as scapegoating turns to abuse.

Like us, at different times in their lives most men exhibit "magical thinking" that states, "If I am like Dad, then Dad will really love and approve of me." This can mean copying his behavior in every way, even if this means becoming abusive.

When sons are young, they are impressionable and pick up all the subtle, as well as not so subtle, nuances of their fathers. Children are very sensitive not just to the words between Dad and Mom, but also the feelings. Many boys see their fathers treat women poorly. Instead of dealing with stress at work or at home, they take it out on others; too often it's women. Sons learn from their fathers how to express unsaid emotions with "looks that could kill." Some learn to be afraid of their anger and deal with anger passive-aggressively, for example, by withdrawing from discussions or by always being late.

Unfortunately, many sons learn from their fathers how to treat a woman as if she were an object, a person to be used, to wait on you, and then be discarded. We have spoken to many sons who learned to hate their fathers for verbally and physically abusing their mothers, and then became just like them as adults.

Though neither of us have ever been physically abusive, we both know what it is like to be overcome with rage that we sometimes directed at women. It was always a part of us that we wanted to stop. We wanted to change our behavior. But for so long, it was too frightening to go inside to find, conquer, and heal the demon within. We have found that healing our relationship has been enormously helpful. It has not only caused us to change how we act toward the women in our lives, but has opened our hearts to a deeper form of intimacy than we ever dreamed possible.

Father as Womanizer

All through our popular culture, there are images of men using and dominating women. This can be very confusing, particularly for young sons. Even fathers who treat women fairly and equally may at times demonstrate something different to their sons. With the high rate of fatherless homes, the covert message to sons and daughters is that a father impregnates the mother and leaves, with no interest in the children. Though the sons of these fathers may be very angry inside, it is common for them to grow up and do the same thing.

The following are excerpts from some of our letters:

Dear Dad,

I realize these are my perceptions and based only on my memory. As I recall, right after the divorce, you dated very actively. I saw you exploring your newfound freedom. You were not with a different woman every week, but just the idea of you being with other women was strange and difficult for me. Since I don't remember you talking to me about any of this, when these various women came in and out of your life, I was not sure if you had any particular emotional feelings. I was not sure if I did either. (Actually, I can only remember a few different women. Perhaps even just a few was a hundred to my unconscious.)

There is also a question I have often wondered, but avoided for the last 25 years or so. Did you have any affairs while you and Mom were married? I have always been faithful to Carny, but this was not always the case for me in other relationships.

Twenty-plus years have passed since the time of the divorce, yet I am amazed at the confusion and anxiety I feel when I ask you this question about your faithfulness. I think I have always hoped that you and Mom were faithful, but have assumed that you were not. For a long time, I hoped I would be faithful, but assumed that I would not be. I'm not even sure why it matters if you were faithful. Judging by my avoidance of the question, it does matter. I do not see myself as a jealous person today, but it is painful to think about the possibility of my wife ever being with someone else. I wonder if some of this is not unconsciously tied with what may never had been talked about with you and Mom.

Also, I want to acknowledge that today I see you as very committed and very honest in your relationship with Diane. I see you treat her as an equal partner in all that you do.

Love,
Lee

Dear Lee,

Thank you for your letter. My recollection was that for a couple months after your mom and I split up I tried to throw myself into my work. The idea of attempting to date seemed abhorrent to me. I wanted to develop a new interest and took a course in photography. For a year I only took pictures of trees. At that time, trees symbolized loneliness, stability, wisdom, and spirituality for me.

Lee, I found myself in agonizing loneliness. Although I thought I wanted to be by myself, I found I hated to be alone. Because I am so bashful it was hard for me to get up the nerve to date. Despite this, I dated a number of different women, most of them being quite a bit younger than I. During that time I did treat women as sex objects. After about six months I saw the craziness of my behavior. Then I began to go in the other extreme and for about six months I lived the life of a monk.

As crazy as it may sound, when I was seeing a lot of women, I was living out my unlived adolescence for the first time. I was also afraid of women because I feared they'd reject me if they got to know the real me. These brief, primarily sexual relationships left me feeling extremely empty inside, and even more alone. My drinking became worse than ever.

Lee, it is difficult to tell you, but I know you want to know: I was not completely faithful to your mom. During the last year of our twenty-year marriage and during our periods of separation, I had three brief affairs. It was a guilt-ridden time where I felt I failed in my marriage, failed my kids, and failed life.

In attempting to answer you, I began to relive some of the pain I carried during the marriage to your mom and some of the pain I inflicted on her. I really feel blessed that most of the time your mom and I have been able to let go of the past and have a warm, loving relationship. I also have at times blamed myself for any difficulties in relationships that you have had. My ego says that if I had been a different model for you, you would not experience any pain in relationships.

Please know that I love you. You and your family are in my prayers each day.

Love,
Dad

The Challenge to Change Our Beliefs

We feel very fortunate to have the goal of attaining truly equal relationships with women. This is not to say we have never been threatened or that it has always been easy to open ourselves up to this new (for us) way of relating. But, curiously, we have seen that healing our relationship with each other has allowed us to feel less threatened in general. Our relationships are not perfect, but we feel we are now on a path of forming closer and more loving connections with both men and women.

Embracing our strength and power and gentleness and vulnerability, has helped us to be more comfortable with both genders. When we focus on compassion, caring, and respect, instead of judgment, criticism, and power struggles, we find much more depth and meaning in every area of life.

Having equal relationships, filled with mutual respect, is what we are striving to achieve. We want to create a safe environment where our children can talk with us about anything, to share their problems and confusions but also their joy. We want to have more time to be with our sons and daughters. All of this may sound obvious, but saying it often and reminding ourselves of our highest priorities is important; otherwise they are only wishes that never become reality.

PART THREE

Healing the Wound

I can be hurt by nothing but my thoughts.

A COURSE IN MIRACLES, (SECOND EDITION, WORKBOOK LESSON 281)

EIGHT

Facing Our Anger

Even if we believe our anger is justified,
it will never bring us peace of mind.

Anger is caused by frustration over the fact that the world is not made to satisfy our desires. Anger is thus inescapable, with us in the cradle and with us as we face our death. If we are human, we get angry. Even Jesus and Gandhi got angry.

JOHN LEE, *FACING THE FIRE*

Dear Lee,

You asked if I was aware that I sit on my anger when I am relating to you. The answer is "yes." A couple of months ago you were discussing the possibility of cutting down on your practice because of your hearing problem. I didn't know that you had gone to the extent of getting such a thorough medical diagnosis when I raised the question about considering additional consultation on your hearing.

You became very angry with me. There was a part of me that felt you were going through a difficult time with loads of fear. There was another part of me that felt my intention was only to be helpful and when you became angry with me, there was a fleeting tendency on my part to become angry with you in return. I chose not to show my anger and sat on it. I told myself to be careful not to push your buttons and not to talk about your hearing unless you directly invited me to discuss it with you.

Lee, as a kid I was always afraid of other people's anger. I was fearful of what it could do. I was afraid rage could make people actually kill each other. That is what I thought when I heard my parents arguing and fighting with each other.

I learned to be very fearful about anger and most of my childhood I tended to stuff my own anger inside of me. I think I did such a good job of denying my own angry feelings that I lost my own awareness of them.

I would guess that in those early years people would have seen me as a very shy child who never talked very much. They would have probably seen me as a very obedient child. I believe others would probably have seen me as a kid who would always obey his parents, almost never risking giving them a bad time or saying what I felt. I think people saw me as a nice kid, well-mannered and disciplined, the kind of kid who was always focused on pleasing others and who would not dare get into trouble.

I would imagine that most people probably missed the fact that under this costume of a well behaved little boy was a kid who was filled with fear and terror, afraid to be angry and show his feelings, and who was always on guard about what awful thing is going to happen next.

I remember some teachers who the kids nicknamed "Old Battle Ax." These were teachers that seemed to be angry all the time. Their tempers had short fuses. Their tongues were so sharp that within seconds they could cut kids into a million pieces. They were not above slapping and spanking kids. I am sure the other kids were also frightened by these teachers, but I always thought my fears were greater than anyone else's.

So I was not a child who showed his anger. All my anger went into internal volcanoes, kept hidden from the outside world. I grew up to be this adult who was afraid of anger. I spent tremendous energy denying my own feelings. I felt so unaccepting of myself—and fearful of rejection—that I became an expert at sensing what would please other people. There was something inside me that thought if I could please other people and get them to like me, they would not get angry or reject me.

I was president of my senior class in high school and president of my medical class at Stanford. In those days, I don't think anyone ever saw me angry. Although I never have thought of myself as an actor, I guess I became a good one.

I became a well-respected psychiatrist and very active in community work. In my office I was always kind, tolerant, loving, and compassionate. But as difficulties developed in my marriage, I became Dr. Jekyll and Mr. Hyde. As you well know, my personality could be quite the opposite at home.

I began to have a temper and I was very inconsistent. I could be very loving and kind and within a moment be just the opposite.

In a strange way I found myself in arguments with your mom in a similar way to what I had observed with my parents. Like my dad, I frequently felt like a victim. I was doing the very thing I was determined not to do. In looking back I feel that one of the dynamics going on with me was I was having overwhelming guilt and fear about my unstated anger.

So what did I do? I developed intolerable pain from back trouble. I unconsciously punished myself. The physicians said I had an organic condition, a degenerated disc. This helped me with my denial and I could tell everyone that this was an organic condition—hiding from others and myself that my guilt about my anger had much to do with my pain.

When I started to become a student of *A Course in Miracles,* I had a faulty picture of what a spiritual person was supposed to look like. That was a picture of someone that was never angry. So I used the workbook lessons to further deny and bury my angry feelings. As time passed, I have become more successful at embracing my anger without projecting it on others. I no longer feel guilty when I feel my anger rise.

A few years ago I came back from a month's retreat in Australia. I discovered in the quiet of nature that I still had a number of withholds in my relationship with Diane. I came back and decided to be more real about what I was feeling. Diane says the next few months were the roughest ones in our marriage. But we did come through it together. Our relationship is now more honest and clear than it has ever been.

I think a few things have happened to me. In my life I am more in the present and much more aware of the feelings going on inside of me. With inner peace as my only goal, I find that I don't get angry that often anymore. It has been very helpful for me to learn to see other people as fearful rather than attacking.

In recent times it has been my impression that, more often than not, you and I have given each other expanded space to express our emotions, our anger, and our frustrations. My perception is that we have both made an effort to stop trying to control the other, which has resulted in deepened feelings of mutual acceptance and friendship. Thank you, Lee, for your part in that gift.

Love,
Dad

Dear Dad,

Through the years I have made a lot of progress in appropriately expressing anger, but I still run into difficulties. I hope that no one who reads this thinks we are experts at dealing with anger and painful emotions. Today in most situations I feel comfortable with anger. But I must admit I can still become confused and tight when anger enters my consciousness. At these times, despite participating in and offering many workshops on anger, I am still not always sure of the best way to approach it. Let me tell you a little of my history in regard to anger.

As I have mentioned before, I grew up being told I had a bad temper. All I knew was that it did not take much for me to explode. Because I was punished for these episodes I quickly learned this was unacceptable. I learned this from you, Mom, school, relatives, and the culture as a whole. Unfortunately nobody ever offered me an alternative to my explosive anger.

Like most kids, I was never taught any ways of communicating or expressing my anger. I learned from Mom that I should be sensitive and caring. Though I am grateful for this, it did not leave much room for anger. I learned from you about internalizing anger. As a result, the combined message I received was "stuff your anger and never show it." I was not very good at this. Much of my life I experienced this cycle: stuff, stuff, explode; stuff, stuff, explode.

When I was 18 I found myself in a public rage in a bar in Sun Valley, Idaho. I was jealous that my girlfriend was with some other guy. I was so embarrassed about this display of rage that I told myself I would never be angry again. For the next several years I stuffed and re-stuffed anger whenever it came up. I thought this was dealing with my anger. Similar to you, the main way I stuffed my anger was with drugs and alcohol.

In my own psychotherapy and many encounter groups in the seventies, I was encouraged to rage, hit pillows, and scream at a chair while pretending someone I was angry at was there. I also learned to write letters to people I was angry with, but never actually mailing them. The idea was that we must reach a catharsis to get rid of our anger. I ended up better able to give myself permission to have my anger, but I was still just as angry.

In the late seventies I began a spiritual path. Here I interpreted that anger was to be released. Through acknowledging the depth of anger and choosing to ask God to take it and give me a different perception, I was able to experience more peace. But I had the nagging feeling that maybe I was denying my anger by spiritualizing and intellectualizing it, on the premise that anger was a bad emotion.

One truth I have learned: We must each find our own solution to anger. There is no one approach for everybody. When we spoke of this recently you were helpful when you suggested that one person may need to beat a pillow for their anger, while another may need to acknowledge the existence of their anger while asking guidance for a different perception. Another way of dealing with anger is, of course, exactly what you and I have been doing in these letters.

I want peace of mind more than anything else. This is why I am writing to you, Dad. In the past I have been so angry with you, I had no idea what to do. I bet that for at least 15 years I could not think about you without having some anger come up. I have delved into that anger, felt it, expressed it, repressed it, carried it, and processed it. Now, at last, I am talking to you about it.

In writing this book, I feel I have finally become ready to let go my anger with you. I am simply ready to release it. I wasn't before. A couple of decades of holding on to anger is long enough.

I want to acknowledge that there is a part of me which says there is no end to my anger. There is murderous rage and an abusive temper waiting to explode. Right now it does not feel beneficial to wallow in this, but rather to acknowledge and release, while asking for a different perception that will lead to peace of mind.

I am tired of being pissed off at you. In my life I have taken my anger toward you and hidden it, projected it, raged with it, controlled with it, and intimidated with it. I have been righteous with it, ashamed by it, processed it, felt powerful with it, and destroyed with it. I have repressed it, exploded with it, and imploded with it. Now I am ready to release it.

In the past I have heard my patients say that they do not want to experience their anger. What's the use? I have urged these people to explore their fears of anger and process it. In the back of my mind, when I looked at my own anger, I wondered if maybe they were right. Perhaps anger was best left alone. Deep inside I did not believe this. Now I feel I have found the place that feels right. It is important that we experience our anger toward our fathers and not keep it hidden out of fear. But it is also imperative that we work toward a willingness to release it and have peace as our single goal.

I've found that the part of us that holds onto anger usually thinks in degrees: "I am a little angry or a little guilty." This is like being a little pregnant—either you are or you aren't. Holding onto a little anger or a little guilt has the same affect as holding onto it all: we cannot fully experience forgiveness and love.

In my relationship with you, I have often been very confused about what I want. I thought if I held on to my anger toward you long enough, maybe one day you would change. Even after you changed, I kept my anger alive by calling you a hypocrite. It is clear that there's a shadowy part of me that will always find a way to keep anger going.

Buddhist teacher Thich Nhat Hanh suggests that if we are present with an emotion *without being taken by it*, we will experience consistent peace of mind. When we are angry, breathe in and say "I am angry," then exhale and say, "I am still angry." When we are no longer angry, we become present with what is there in that new moment. This has been very helpful to me because it is the authentic ground that lies between my encounter group catharsis and spiritual denial.

I hope that you and I continue to be honest about our anger when it comes up. It has been very freeing to be able to express it to you without fear of you shutting off our relationship. I know we had to start slowly with this process to feel each other out, but now it feels like I can share anger with you when it comes up. As I write this to you, I am aware I am not sure you feel the same toward me. You have expressed a great deal to me, but I have wondered if you sit on anger and other emotions because you are afraid of my reaction.

Recently, something came up that I see as a source of some of my past anger. I found that while growing up, a catch-22 was the source of some of my anger. It dawned on me that I wanted to please and be accepted by both you and Mom. To be accepted by you, I thought I should be like you. But Mom, like many mothers, tried to cultivate characteristics in me that she did not have in her relationship with you. I ended up feeling torn inside. I would have to abandon you to fulfill Mom's goals for me, and would have to abandon her to be like you. I remember when Mom was really mad at me she would say, "You're just like your father." In the end, I felt I couldn't be accepted by both of you and so I became angry at both of you.

In closing, I want you to know that I will always do my best to listen and not become defensive. And I want you to know that if I do become defensive or withdrawn, I will come back and get on track. Our relationship is too important to me to let anger have any permanence.

Love,
Lee

The Importance of Solitude

I (Lee) once took a short workshop on healing the relationship with one's parents. After two hours, we took a break. As we left the room where the workshop was being held, I happened to notice that the line at the phone booth was about ten deep. These people were on the phone calling their parents to confront them with all of the shame they had "caused" them.

Though there is certainly value to opening communication

with your parents, there is also value in spending time with yourself before doing so. We hope this book will help heal your relationship with your father, but we also hope it will assist you in developing a deeper relationship with your self.

In the past, each of us had great difficulty spending any time alone. It seemed that depression and/or anxiety would often surface if we spent more than an hour by ourselves. This was partially because we had so many repressed feelings and solitude was a door to these feelings which we didn't want to open. For many men aloneness can lead to a fear of the unknown, of a deep void within.

There was a part of us that made solitude something very fearful, that it should be avoided because the following cycle would occur if we were alone and not busy for any period:

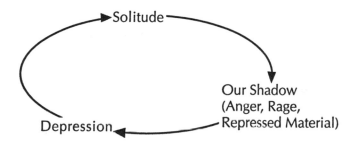

In our healing it has been important for us to spend time in solitude; this is where we can begin exploring and confronting our fear and unhappiness. We found talking to each other is important but insufficient. If we don't also spend time quietly with ourselves, we miss the opportunity for increased self-awareness.

We found that for us, a mixture of both *solitude* and *communication* led to the most healing. We know now that if we don't run from the initial discomfort solitude can initiate, then solitude can actually bring the following cycle into being:

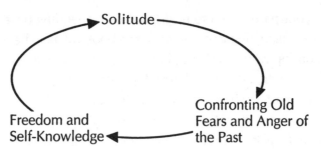

We also found that attempting to spend at least half of a day in solitude every few weeks was important to us. During this time we would not read, go to the movies, or have any form of outside stimulus or entertainment. Instead we would walk, sit, meditate, or write in a journal. We just spent time with ourselves. We reminded ourselves often—*you would never expect to develop a deep relationship with somebody that you never spent any time with.* The same is true in your relationship with yourself.

Anger and Guilt

It is painful to admit, but our love/hate relationship with each other served to cover the experience of love and the presence of God. Many sons (including us) project on their fathers the concept of a God that rewards if you are good and punishes if you are bad. When our fathers reject, criticize, punish, or abandon us, it is like God abandoning us. When we were growing up, we both frequently felt that we must have done something terrible to make us so unworthy of love. As long as we chose to believe this, we increased our levels of blame, anger, and guilt.

When we began working on our father issues, the first feeling to emerge was anger. As we worked through our anger, the next and overwhelming feeling was usually guilt. We found that our guilt came from our belief that it was our fault our fathers were the way they were. In talking to other men, we have found we are not alone. Even when it makes absolutely no intellectual sense, sons go on carrying this guilt through their lives.

In a workshop we conducted, we were working with a 14-year-old boy who felt very out of place in the room full of older men. To make him feel more a part of the group, we said to the group, "Quickly, what is the first thing that comes to your mind? You're 14 years old and you're going to say one thing to your dad from your gut, without the fear of retaliation of any kind." These are some of the statements that we heard from thirty men:

Get off my ass.

You son of a bitch.

You hit first every time, you never tell me what you think or feel.

I want to fill your shoes, but I want to do it my way.

You're all work and no play.

Listen to me.

Let me in.

Tell me that you care.

Don't bother me.

You are such a weakling. Why don't you stand up to Mom?

It's not my fault.

Stop being angry with me all of the time.

If you keep doing that to me, I am going to kill you some day when I'm big enough.

You have no idea how I feel. You don't even know who I am.

Let me cry.

Let me choose for myself.

These statements came from the mouths of men who left being 14 years old many decades ago, yet still carried the anger of their youth. A statement made by one of the men reflects the carried guilt. The proclamation, "It is not my fault" is our unconscious actually screaming "I feel so guilty. It is my fault that you are not here more. What did I do wrong? I just want to fix it."

Chuck (father) and John (son) were in another one of our workshops together. John was 35 years old and this was the second day of seeing his father since his father left the house 28 years ago. The following is a partial exchange they had. Though their situation was quite different than ours, we found what they were saying mirrored much of our feelings in the past. Their exchange illustrates the universal guilt that fathers and sons carry when the father is either physically or emotionally absent.

JOHN: I really never thought seriously about contacting you until a couple of months ago. I just ... It's really hard to define ... I just need to understand why you left. I need to understand what a father is, because I never had one and now I am one. Dad, what do you see as the role of you being my father?

CHUCK: When you were young I never even thought about it. I was drinking and working. What I feel today is that being a father is being a teacher to the son to become an honorable person—to teach openness and acceptance. Even though I did not teach you these things, I am happy to see them in you.

JOHN: Dad, I did not even know that I was angry until coming here today. It is hard to explain how I feel. You left and I've never known why. All I have thought is, it was just that we moved. Someone turned off the switch and you were gone. That was it. I felt abandoned. Dad, why did you abandon me?

CHUCK: Because the only thing I could think of at that time was myself. I could not see beyond my own needs. I am very deeply sorry. I try to forgive myself. Most of the time I think that I have, but right now I just don't know.

JOHN: It's not so much anger I feel right now listening to you. It's resentment. I felt left out.

CHUCK: One time I wanted to see you, to make contact, but your mother told me that you never wanted to see me again. So I never tried again. I suppose that I should have. I have always felt guilty that I didn't keep in contact with you. But after a while I just thought that you didn't want to see me.

[After a lot of dialogue, John said the following.]

JOHN: I just wanted you to be there. All the way through school you were never there. When I was in high school I started to close up. I just tried to forget. It was hard. Kids would ask me about my dad. I would just say, "My dad is gone. I don't know where he is." I would feel confused, angry, and blame myself. I don't know, it just seemed like it was my fault you and Mom split up and we moved.

We then said to John, "Twenty-nine years of blaming yourself. That's a hell of a long time. Would you like to hear from your dad in more detail what led to your parents splitting up and more details about why he left?" John said he would.

What transpired was further heart-felt dialogue about the feelings of both father and son. They were both able to see how much guilt they had carried. It is always a remarkable experience to see such ancient wounds begin to heal. They both left that day with the commitment to each other to continue their relationship. Chuck said: "I come from a family that never talked. So if there is one thing that has been deafening around me, it has been my silence. I need to communicate to you my love and continue to affirm that I love you. This is not easy for me, and I will often need your help. I want you to know that I will be as available as I know how to be, and this will never change. I want you to be honest with your feelings. Though sometimes it may be hard for me to listen, nothing that you say will make me go away again. Not ever."

Blocks to the Expression of Anger and Other Difficult Feelings

For us to begin expressing our true feelings, it was helpful to ask ourselves the following questions:

- Do I have feelings toward my father (and others) that I have never expressed?
- Does keeping anger and other emotions inside affect me in any negative ways?
- How would my life and relationships be different if I felt free to express these feelings to another person?
- Is there any positive purpose to keeping my feelings buried?
- What would it be like to have anger toward my father on the day I die?
- Do my feelings of justified anger get me what I really want?
- Does holding onto anger bring me peace of mind?
- Am I afraid that if I become consciously aware of my angry feelings that I will no longer be able to control them?
- Am I afraid I could end up physically hurting another person?

There were many experiences we each had as children that built beliefs leading to repression and denial of difficult feelings. We have found this to be true for many men. (For a list that identifies some of these beliefs and experiences, see Going Further.)

Our beliefs had a common theme: they kept us from being closer to each other. They also kept us from experiencing much intimacy with others. Most importantly, they kept us from relating to the inner processes of our own selves. We not only became distant from our outside world, we also became alienated from our own inner life.

As a result of a transformational encounter or near-death experience, it is not uncommon for a father of adult or adolescent sons to make a big transition in how they relate to their sons. This was true for my (Lee) dad. When my dad had a spiritual transformation, he realized he wanted a different relationship with his sons. He began to be more available, but I was very weary. On one hand I was glad to see Dad change, but I did not trust it. Before I could let him in, I had to let go of the resentment I still held within me, for all the years I needed him and he wasn't there. For me it was not a short process, I first had to discover my own identity.

How To Begin Experiencing and Communicating Feelings

In looking back at what has been helpful in improving our relationship, we found that when dealing with anger and other uncomfortable feelings toward each other, it has been important to address the seven aspects of our communication. Though we did not always do so, it is usually beneficial to address these within ourselves or with the help of a therapist or friend, before we even begin to talk with the other person. When we did not do this, it was easy to become confused and adopt attacking and defensive behavior.

We found that dumping our anger on each other was not the best way of processing our anger. We did find, however, that when we took responsibility for our own emotions and experiences, without the hook of blame, we could safely express our feelings with each other. We reminded ourselves of Workbook Lesson 281 from *A Course in Miracles,* "I can be hurt by nothing but my thoughts."

To express our feelings, we had to allow ourselves to openly communicate. There are seven aspects of communication that need to be understood before we can do that. They are:

1. Unspoken expectations
2. Unspoken assumptions
3. What inhibits our expression of feeling
4. Abuse
5. Obstacles to love
6. Personal responsibility (ceasing to be a victim)
7. Acknowledgment and acceptance

Following are short sections on each of these seven aspects. At the end of each section there is a statement to contemplate. We found it helpful to complete these statements by writing in a journal. As we approached these seven aspects, it was important for us not to worry whether the other person would be there to listen to us. It is an extremely valuable exercise to complete even if it is never to be shared.

Although this does not closely resemble the original, I (Lee) have adapted this exercise from one I first saw in a training at Scripps Hospital in San Diego.

Aspect 1: Unspoken Expectations

One of the main sources of problems in our relationship was our unspoken expectations of each other. As we began to look closely at our expectations, we found that most were either not realistic, or reflected our own unresolved issues. We also saw that some of our expectations were reasonable and positive (I expect you to tell me the truth) while other expectations were unreasonable and negative (I expect you to always be able to give me what I want).

In looking closely at how I (Lee) related to my dad growing up I found I had opposing expectations. Our egos are experts at creating opposing expectations that make peace of mind impossible. As an adolescent I expected my Dad to be more involved in my life. I wanted ongoing guidance. I also expected him to leave me alone and not to tell me what to do all of the time. These opposing expectations are typical of a teenager and create a no-win situation for the father. Unfortunately, like many sons, I carried these opposing expectations into my adulthood.

It was important that we recognize many of our childhood desires were impossible to fulfill. We discovered a little boy within us that wants our father to be a man that holds every positive characteristic we can imagine and freely offers us constant validation and acceptance. We wanted Dad to be an athlete, intellectual, ecologist, artist, and a mechanic. We wanted him to show us all of these different worlds. We wanted him to be more like John's dad, Peter's dad, and Al's dad, who were all very different from one another. We wanted him to be directive, decisive, and a sensitive and compassionate companion. Our unconscious list is never-ending and we must recognize an important fact: Our fathers are human and will never be able to fulfill all of our archetypal expectations.

Complete the following sentence with both positive and negative expectations that you have for your father or son.

In our relationship, I expect of/from you_____.

Aspect 2: Unspoken Assumptions

Assumptions block intimacy and prevent effective communication. When we assume something about each other or assume that the other knows how we feel, we create a reality that may not be even close to accurate. For us, assumptions kept us stuck in the same negative patterns of thinking and behaving.

Most father and son relationships we have encountered are not very different from ours. They are built on assumptions rather than on any clear and consistent communication. If fathers and sons are not verbally saying how they feel toward each other, rest assured that assumptions are being built.

As we began to clarify, communicate, and develop a willingness to release our expectations of one another, we can begin to establish real relationships with each other.

Complete the following statement with assumptions that you have about your father or son. Include both positive assumptions (I assume that you know that I love you) and painful memories (I assume that you know the depth of my feelings of abandonment when you and Mom divorced).

I assume that you know_____.

Aspect 3: What Inhibits Our Expression of Feeling

When we experience emotional pain, the tendency is to become guarded. We don't want to get hurt again. Our desire to keep ourselves safe from repeating the past, resulted in our avoiding many issues and topics with each other. Some of our pain and guilt originated a very long time ago, yet was never discussed. Until we talked about it, we still carried it with us.

Through the years our communication became strained and shallow. We kept secrets, sometimes even from ourselves, and we never let ourselves be known to the other person. In turn, our relationships with others also became limited.

Think of some topics that you avoid talking about with your father or son, or feelings that are uncomfortable for you to discuss. Then complete the following two statements about your father or son.

These are some of the topics I hesitate to bring up with you_____.

I have difficulty sharing these feelings with you_____.

Aspect 4: Abuse

Physical and emotional abuse is a reality in many families. We recognize that our relationships have suffered and been complicated by our past drug and alcohol use. It has been extremely difficult to take a close look at the forms of abuse in our father–son relationship because it is something that we would like to forget.

Usually whenever there has been abuse, there is tremendous anger, guilt, and shame. Our guilt and shame kept us quiet, and we built prisons of despair deep within our psyche. The saddest part is that until we began to talk about and heal abuse, we were likely to repeat the pattern. Where applicable, complete the following six statements.

My use of drugs and/or alcohol has affected our relationship in these ways_____.

Your use of drugs and alcohol has affected our relationship in these ways_____.

As a son, some of my most painful memories of you are_____.

As a father, some of my most painful memories of you are_____.

As a father, what I have the most guilt about is_____.

As a son, what I have the most guilt about is_____.

Aspect 5: Obstacles to Love

In our heart of hearts, we wanted a close and healed relationship. Yet when we were honest with ourselves, we realized that we did not know what created closeness or distance in our relationship. We needed to identify this.

To identify the obstacles to love we had with each other, it was helpful for us to think about the times when we felt fearful and distant with one another. To identify what would lead to healing, we would think about times when we felt close and connected. We began to ask ourselves what was going on in our thinking during these different times.

Complete the following about your father or son. Include both behavior (I feel distant from you when you interrupt me before I finish talking) and statements that reflect your thinking (I feel close to you when I accept you for who you are).

I feel distant from you when_____.

I feel close to you when_____.

Aspect 6: Personal Responsibility

Once we decided to stop being victims and began asking ourselves what we could do to heal, our lives almost magically became more alive and full. Neither of us wanted to become like so many sons we saw who went to their grave carrying a chip on their shoulders about their fathers, nor did we want to be like many fathers before us who died feeling guilty about the type of fathers they had been.

We made the conscious decision that we were not going to be victims any longer. We made the decision to heal. To make these decisions, we did not have to know how to go about doing it or even believe it was possible. To initiate the healing process all we needed to do was to decide we wanted to heal. Our conscious decision was enough to direct our mind toward healing.

Healing our relationship required us to make a deep commitment to ourselves to work on the relationship. Each of us recognized that the other person did not have to reciprocate this commitment or be present for us to move toward healing. We have primarily worked with our thoughts, memories, feelings, and beliefs.

Some things we have done to improve our relationship have been behavioral (I will spend more time with you) and others have been internal (I will try to work through and release blame). We also have slowly realized that the other person did not have to change for healing to occur. When we were stuck in that belief, we continued to be victims.

Complete the following, stating both internal and external changes.

In order to improve our relationship, I am willing to
_____.

Aspect 7: Acknowledgment and Acceptance

In our relationship our positive traits often went unrecognized by ourselves and each other. Letting it be known what we value in ourselves is an important part of healing our relationship.

Sometimes we assumed the other person knew what we liked about ourselves. At times, we also assumed that our fathers/sons didn't think there was anything about us to like because we felt we never pleased them.

At times in our relationship it has been easier for us to share our negative views of ourselves and each other. It has been important that we each acknowledge the positive traits we see in ourselves. It has been equally important for us to share these with each other.

Complete the following statement.

I value these traits in myself_____.

Just as we assumed that we each knew how the other felt, we often made the faulty assumption that we didn't need to directly verbalize positive traits about them. As sons, we noticed a tendency to spend much more time thinking about all the characteristics we did not like about our fathers. To help in accepting the whole person, it has been important for us to think about and verbalize the positive.

We recognize that some fathers were so abusive that their son's immediate response would be, "There was nothing good about that son of a bitch." Or with fathers that were absent the response may be, "I never knew my father. How would I know what he is like?" In these cases we suggest that for the purpose of this exercise you picture your father as a young and inno-cent boy. Imagine what his potential and positive traits might have been then.

It was also helpful for us to recognize cultural differences between the time our dad was fathering and now. Today we expect much more from fathers. Some years ago being a good provider, not being abusive or a drunk, and paying minimal attention to the kids for a few hours on Sunday was about all it took to be seen as a good father. Today the list is forever grow-ing: change diapers, be sensitive and understanding to feel-ings, support emotionally, pick up the kids from school, make dinner. When you look back at how your father was, take the era into consideration. Don't just judge him with the measur-ing stick of the ideal nineties dad.

We found that communicating the positive traits we saw in each other was just as important as communicating all of the negative traits. These are the things we need to hear most from each other and yet we often say the least.

Complete the following statement.

The traits that I most value in you are_____.

The Courage to Stay with the Process of Healing

It is easy to give up. Many times in the process of healing, our own pain and memories seemed too much to overcome. There have also been times when we each tried to talk to each other and were met with anger and rejection. At these times, it seemed futile to continue.

One thing we have found to be true is if we stay with our inner process, rather than repressing it, we can and will move through the pain and into freedom. As we confront and explore our own shadow, that is, the things we'd rather keep hidden, we can use our experience to join with other people in our lives.

We have both discovered that once anger is dealt with and the repressed material is brought out of the darkness and worked through, we can begin to deepen our relationships with our fathers, ourselves, and God. We are never quite done with this because depth is infinite. As Jerrold Shapiro states about his relationship with his father in *The Measure of a Man,* "I cannot think of anything particular that I have left unsaid, yet know down deep that there is much more." For us, the "much more" is not necessarily more material to process, it is more depth and intimacy to discover. Writing this book together and discovering the love we have for each other has been part of this "much more."

NINE

Forgiveness,
the Great Healer

*Forgiveness means giving up
all thoughts for a better past.*

ANONYMOUS

I can't forget the past and all the disappointments I experienced as a child. They are part of the fabric of my life. Yet I can stop blaming my father for what I never received. He loved me as he was able. Life is too short to allow past hurts to ruin the beauty of the present. My father is precious to me, and through him I am linked forever to all men back to the beginning of human history.

JED DIAMOND, *THE WARRIOR'S JOURNEY HOME*

Dear Lee,

When I was growing up, I don't remember the word "forgiveness" being used very much in our household. I doubt if it was a word I would have known how to define, let alone spell. In my limited perception it seemed there was considerable talk about finding fault and blame. Even as a young child it seemed that everything I did was wrong.

I was clumsy, the guy who was always spilling the milk. It never seemed like I could live up to my parent's expectations for me. I remember my mom held grudges against many people. When I was writing the book *Out of Darkness Into the Light*, she asked me what the book was about. I replied, "It's about forgiveness." She turned to me and looked me right in the eye and stated, "If you are going to keep writing those books on forgiveness I am going to write a book called *The Importance of Being Unforgiving*."

My dad, on the other hand, did not hold grudges, and I could never imagine anyone not liking him. He did not seem to hold the shadow of the past with those who came across his path in life. Perhaps his gentleness was his strongest trait.

In spite of this, there was one disappointment that I believe he had with me all his life. Dad's life was his date store. He, with my mom, worked extremely hard and long hours to make it a success. He wanted very much for my two older brothers to take it over and keep the family business going. Well, as you know Les became a chemist and Art became an ophthalmologist. I was the youngest by six years.

Dad did everything he could to convince me to take over the store. I believe his greatest dream was to see that this business he and Mom had built would be kept in the family. I was his last hope. Although a part of me wanted to please him, I knew that selling dates would never bring me joy. As a matter of fact, I ended up hating dates.

Lee, there is no way for me to share with you the disappointment that I remember in my dad's face when I told him I wanted to go to college and become a psychiatrist. As I said, Dad was not one to hold a grudge, but in my mind I still question if he ever totally forgave me. I think all through my life I've felt a twinge of guilt that Dad would have been happier if I had made the decision to take over the family store.

In looking back at my childhood, I felt that mistakes were not allowed and that almost everyone was constantly finding fault with me. I guess it is not to difficult to understand why I in turn became somewhat of an expert at finding fault with others. Unfortunately this continued into my adult life.

Little did I realize then that all the fault-finding and the unforgiving thoughts I had about others were really just projections of my unforgiving thoughts about myself. I felt, as I imagine you must have felt at times, that if my parents had really loved and accepted me in the way I needed, then I would not have had to face all the problems I encountered in life.

As a kid I felt I was the cause of everything that went wrong in the family. I felt that if I had performed better in school and been a better peacemaker at home, many of the troubles our family had would have disappeared. I guess I have always had a stubborn streak because for most of my life it has been very hard for me to forgive myself.

Sometimes I when I think about not being there for you in your childhood, I have felt like a real sinner who deserves guilt and punishment for the rest of my life. At the time of your mom's and my divorce, I experiences a lot of rage, anger, and blame. There was also a part of me that felt I was deserting you. I felt in a double bind: you would be emotionally hurt if I stayed and emotionally hurt if I left. I was a prisoner of my guilt either way. It took me many years to be willing to forgive myself. I am beginning to believe it is a life-long process.

Since 1975 when I became a student of *A Course in Miracles,* I have done my best to make forgiveness my primary function in life. As you well know I am not always so successful, but I do feel I am becoming more consistent. It never occurred to me before 1975 that forgiveness was the key to happiness.

There were many times in my life when I thought my relationship with your mom would never heal. I was afraid we could never again become friends. Our healed relationship is one of the miracles of my life, proving forgiveness really works. It was something I had thought would be impossible. I didn't realize the real reason I thought it was impossible was because I didn't believe I deserved to be happy and that I didn't deserve your mom's or my own forgiveness.

We teach what we want to learn. All of my books have been on forgiveness because that is what I need to learn so much. I want to see every person in my life as a teacher of forgiveness. Your willingness to reopen the past, not to analyze it to death, but to find another way of looking at the past has been the greatest of gifts for me. I don't think there is any question in both of our minds that we have become very strong teachers of forgiveness to each other. Perhaps the wake-up call for you and I, and for all of us, is that love and forgiveness can be a very practical way of life.

Love,
Dad

Dear Dad,
I am saddened to think how many opportunities for forgiveness have been presented to me, and how often I have

turned away from them. Why have I thought it is safer to hold on to anger with you than release it? How is it that I found any value in blame?

The experience of writing this book has given me another opportunity to forgive and let go, yet this hasn't come easily. There have been moments in this process when I have wanted to throw it away and only have a relationship with you where we talk maybe a couple times a year. Sometimes being distant from you feels safer and freer. Yet what I really know to be true is that wherever I am, my unhealed relationships go with me.

I am happy to say that as we approach the end of this book, I feel very close to you and there is nothing I am still holding onto. I never thought I would be able to say that. It is very freeing.

Am I alone? I have had feelings of overwhelming aloneness, as though nobody would ever know who I am, including myself. I feel known by you right now and that feels surprisingly good. I would not say I always feel understood by you, but being known is different than being understood. I think that sometimes we, like all people, don't hear each other when we are talking and have very different perceptions of events. I have come to see that this is all outer stuff and does not have to do with being deeply known. Some people understand where I am coming from or what I am saying, but do not really know me. You know me—my guts, my heart, and my hopes.

You came to know me by me being able to let you in. I could not let you in until I saw value in forgiving you. *A Course in Miracles* suggests that forgiveness is an illusion, because it has to do with the past. But it also suggests it is the only illusion that leads to peace, because it has to do with releasing the past.

In years to come, when I look at our book sitting on my shelf, it will represent forgiveness. I want others to read this and know that if we can forgive each other, anybody can. Because I think there was a time when both of us thought that forgiveness was an impossibility.

In closing I would like to write a poem to you.

The Paradox of My Father

You have been the poison that I drank daily,
and the sweet elixir of love
surrounding me in magical protection
in my most painful moments.
You have been the bars that imprisoned me,
and the green fields that have freed me.

You have been the cause of my building high walls,
and the source of my taking them down.
Your life has angered and controlled me,
and inspired and released me.
My anger towards you has sent me running
from you and myself
and something deep has been the roots
that pulled and called me back.

We have been magnets that attract,
and magnets that only allow
distant closeness.

Forgiveness allows me now to heal,
to step away from the paradox and join with you.
Dad, beyond all of our history we are the same.
We want love, acceptance, and joining.
Let this be the time when we both choose to see only this.

From this point on, when anger and pain arise,
may we both be willing to acknowledge and release.

I pray the guiding principles in my life with you will be
I'll not hide any dark feelings from you;
I'll have the intent to release them rather than hold on
By seeing the light of God's Love shining in you.
By doing this I will be committing to practicing
forgiveness.

Peace to you, to me,
and to the world,
Lee

Another Way of Looking at the Wound

Let us imagine for a moment that a small boy is stabbed with a knife in the abdomen. He is taken to a hospital where they do exploratory surgery and then suture him up. Months later he develops abdominal pain. The physician discovers that an abscess has formed in the lining of the stomach. (An internal abscess is like a boil on the skin. It is walled off, has puss in its center and all the signs of infection.) The physician removes the abscess surgically and the child is given antibiotics. Very quickly the boy is normal and healthy again.

For both of us, the emotional traumas between us have at times felt like knife wounds going right into our gut. Even though the pain was initially quite acute, we both now recognize how we repressed it. We formed internal emotional abscesses that were walled off from our consciousness.

Our emotional abscesses became infected with fear, anger, grief, and resentment. Our repression was so powerful that for years we numbed ourselves from any conscious awareness of pain. The willingness to forgive has been like the surgical removal of a physical abscess within us. Developing understanding and compassion for each other has been like the antibiotic that slowly heals the wound. We have discovered that the act of forgiveness brings immediate healing.

As you have seen in the letters, there have been many symptoms from our unhealed emotional wounds, brought about by the conflicts between each other and holding on to unforgiving thoughts. For us, fear of intimacy and control issues were symptoms at the top of the list.

For a long time, if you asked us about our feelings about our fathers, our usual reply would have been that we had no problems with our father. Then we would do everything we could to change the subject. If we were in touch with our inner selves at that point in our lives we would probably have told you that we felt unlovable, unconnected to others, and that we didn't know how to love or be loved. We would have told you that we felt spiritually empty.

Lack of Healing

We could not heal our emotional wounds until we were aware we had them. Hanging onto the painful past and recycling it by projecting it into our relationships with others kept us from healing our old wounds.

Like us, most men want to hear from their father: "I love you as you are and I am proud of you just being you. You don't have to be perfect for me to love you." Unfortunately, few men hear these words. Though we were not initially aware of it, we discovered the scars of our childhood were never completely healed and remained as open wounds. Our wounds remained open because they continued to itch and we kept scratching them.

We now clearly see that denying or fighting the old pain does not get rid of it. Our fear of the pain actually prolonged it. This kept our pain stirred up internally and hidden from our conscious awareness.

Why We Don't Forgive

It is important for us to honor that it has taken courage for us to face and embrace the repressed pain and grief that led to our feeling so separate from each other. Getting in touch with and experiencing our anger and fears has helped us release the years of built up, buried inner tension.

At times our egos took up the cause and screamed at us that we must never let go of our pain or the same hurtful, disappointing things would happen again. Our egos wanted us to believe that our fathers caused our pain and that our fathers were unforgivable. If our egos had their way, we would stay in the victim role for the rest of our lives, never experiencing true peace of mind.

In the process of healing, we realized that we went into adult life holding onto justified anger and resentment because we believed we never experienced acceptance and unconditional love from our fathers. In the letters, at some level, we felt angry and guilty because we believed we were never able live up to our dads' expectations: we believed there was something wrong or unlovable about us. Unconsciously we concluded we were the cause of our father's rejection.

In our worst moments, the voice of the ego shouts in our ears that our fathers don't deserve to be forgiven and our continued resentment is justified. What our egos don't tell us is:

When we make the decision to hold onto our grievances and not forgive, we are making the choice to suffer.

Our egos would have us act like we are stuck in revolving doors, condemning our fathers and condemning ourselves.

Once again, we lose either way. Truly, there is no joy in a life based on blame and guilt. One of the songs of the unforgiving heart is, "Anything and everything that goes wrong in my life is my dad's fault. It is his fault that I feel lost and empty inside and that I have lost my way."

Fear and unforgiving thoughts keep our pain and anger alive. When we become attached to our so-called justified anger and unforgiving thoughts, there is no way we can experience peace of mind and the presence of God or higher power.

We have been amazed at how clever our egos are. For years we would both arrange to have many people supporting our unforgiving thoughts about our fathers. The last thing our unforgiving hearts would have us do is take charge of our lives and stop reliving the past. They would not want us to wake up and become aware of the big secret they have kept from us:

There is nobody to blame—not even ourselves.

Our egos give us a thousand reasons why we should never forgive our fathers and why we should never drop our guard and let our fathers come close to us. I (Jerry) came to realize that the result of my unforgiving thoughts was numbness; I pretended I had no feelings and I didn't care.

We have spent a lot of time holding onto illusions that keep healing from us. Here is a list of some of the illusions that tell us not to forgive our fathers:

- What my father did to me deserves my "unforgiveness."
- My father deserves to be punished.
- If I forgive my father, it would be a sign of my weakness.
- If I forgive my father he will just turn around and do the same thing again.
- If I forgive my father it would make him right and me wrong.

- If I forgive my father that would signify that I approved of his behavior.
- Dad never forgave me for any of my wrong doings, so I'll give him back the same medicine.
- The secret of never getting hurt by my father is to never forgive him for what he has done to me.
- Both what Dad did and what he did not do are unforgivable.
- I will have power over my father if I don't forgive.
- Even if my father comes crawling on his hands and knees asking for my forgiveness, it would be stupid on my part to forgive him.
- Don't forgive. The revenge of never forgiving him feels good to my ego.
- When I don't forgive, it covers up and hides responsibility I can now take in the relationship.
- When I don't forgive, it keeps a certainty of distance so I don't have to deal with the risks and uncertainty of intimacy.

The Healing of the Wound

At a workshop Diane and I (Jerry) were giving, I was once told a new definition of forgiveness: *"Forgiveness means letting go of all hopes for a better past."* It is true we cannot change the past; what we can change is our thoughts and attitudes about the past.

It is through healing and releasing the past in our relationship that has given us freedom. Writing this book has helped us out of being stuck in the quicksand that we put ourselves in so many years ago. We still find it helpful to remind ourselves over and over that our willingness to consciously face our pains, fears, and wounds leads to a healing that in turn brings peace of mind.

Forgiveness

We have found in our relationship that we cannot hold onto grievances and experience peace at the same time. Peace and love are inseparable from each other. We cannot experience guilt and love or guilt and peace at the same time. Inner peace, the peace of God, is only experienced in the present.

Both of us tried for years to change our behavior in certain ways. Sometimes we would be successful for short periods, but we were still not very happy. We found that we could not experience deep and meaningful change in our lives until we changed our beliefs and our thoughts. For us, the first step in getting rid of a life of guilt and blame was to no longer see any value in the ego's games. It meant no longer seeing any value in reliving or holding onto the past. To continue healing our relationship, we need a constant willingness to let go of what has happened and see each other in the light of the present moment. We still have times when we become absorbed in the fear, anger, and guilt of the ego. When we fall into the trap of the ego, we try to remember to ask ourselves the following three questions:

1. Do my grievances bring me peace of mind?
2. Does holding onto vengeful feelings and resentment about my father bring me inner peace?
3. Does my continuing to value guilt, blame, and self-condemnation bring me inner peace?

Reminding ourselves that the answer to these questions is "no" helps us to direct our minds towards forgiveness.

Our dear friend, Bill Thetford, who helped Helen Schucman bring *A Course In Miracles* into being, once said "We need to practice celestial amnesia." He defined celestial amnesia as

living a life where all that we remember of the past is the love
we have received and given. When we believe that love is all
that makes up our true reality, this becomes much easier.

As we have said before, our egos never forgive. It is our unforgiving thoughts that keep our egos alive and active. The secret
of forgiveness is to have *just a little willingness* to give all our
anger, rage, shame, and hurtful feelings from the past to God
or our higher power and trust that those feelings will be trans-
formed into love.

For us, forgiveness is what allows us to experience ourselves
as spiritual beings. When we, as father and son, began to share
our vulnerability and our feelings with each other, we began
to forgive. We have found the process of forgiving each other
and ourselves to be nothing short of a spiritual transformation
in our lives.

Forgiveness helps us to rid ourselves of the illusion of separation and permits us to feel a sense of oneness. When we
choose to listen to our heart rather than our heads, we realize
the key to happiness is forgiveness. There is a passage from *A
Course of Miracles* (Workbook Lesson 122) that we have found
helpful in our search to understand how to forgive:

> *Forgiveness offers everything that I want. What could you
> want that forgiveness cannot give? Do you want peace? For-
> giveness offers it. Do you want happiness, a quiet mind, a
> certainty of purpose, and a sense of worth and beauty that
> transcends the world? Do you want care and safety, and
> always the warmth of sure protection? Do you want a quiet-
> ness that cannot be disturbed, a gentleness that never can
> be hurt, a deep, abiding comfort, and a rest so perfect it can
> never be upset?*

All this forgiveness offers you, and more. It sparkles on your eyes as you awake, and gives you joy with which to meet the day. It soothes your forehead while you sleep, and rests upon your eyelids so you will have no dreams of fear and evil, malice and attack. When you awake again, it offers you another day of happiness and peace. Forgiveness offers you all this and more.

Recapturing the Sacredness of the Father–Son Relationship

As you listen more closely to your sacred self and transcend your ego, so too will the world ego be shifted away from power, control, and money back to basic virtues of higher awareness—back to peace, beauty, love, purity, tolerance, patience, and compassion.

DR. WAYNE W. DYER, *YOUR SACRED SELF*

There is a deep cry from within our souls for a life with meaning, a life with love, and a life without fear. The experience of our journey has been difficult to put into words, but we have done our best to convey what is deep within us.

At the end of this writing, we are most aware of feeling what might be described as the holiness and sacredness of our souls' relationship to each other and to God. This is a miracle; as we began this writing process we both had fears we would only become angrier, guiltier, and more distant from each other.

There are still silences between us but they are no longer silences built on fear and anger. These new silences involve cherishing the holiness within each other and ourselves as we mutually reach out to God. This new silence is sacred and filled with love. We have discovered a new world.

A New World

Through being open to healing we have walked into
a world where unconditional love is sacred;
where caring and compassion become our grace;
where forgiveness releases us from our past;
where guilt, fear, and false perceptions
are distant memories of another life;
where we recognize we are one;
where we allow our souls
to join with other souls and their Source.

Forgiveness has helped us clear our life's journey of self-imposed obstacles to love. It has allowed us to experience what is beyond words: the sacredness of our relationship with each other and with God. Forgiveness removes all blocks to the presence of that love which is eternal.

Healing our relationship with each other has enabled us to begin seeing our other relationships as holy encounters. We experience sacredness when we rid ourselves of all our illusions of separation. When we totally forgive our fathers and ourselves, we begin to experience joining and Oneness.

In closing, we have written two more letters, trying to capture the experience of writing this book.

Dear Dad,

Yesterday was Father's Day. It seems an appropriate time to complete this book. Writing it has not been easy for me and yet it has been deeply worthwhile. As I finish this writing with you, I am aware of two things: I am grateful for the healing that working on this book with you has brought; and thank God it's over!

"Recapturing the sacredness of the father and son relationship" sounds as though we should be walking into an eternal sunset joined hand in hand, with nothing but gentleness and light radiating from us. This is far from the truth. So what is this "sacredness" that we have recaptured?

I still have the temptation to push you away when I need you most. There are still times that you plug me into my anger more than anybody else on the planet. There is no doubt that at times I still look to you for validation and approval. There are still occasions when I would rather not deal with you, and still situations when I do not feel heard by you. I suppose that from the initial sound of it nothing has changed, but this is not true. My experience of you, me, us, and God has evolved greatly in our journey of healing.

The primary change is that I have recognized how important you are to me, and how deep into my unconscious our relationship goes. Embracing this has given me patience and tolerance for me, you, and us together. With patience I have found new perceptions that have allowed me to let go of past hurts. Embracing the importance of our relationship, developing patience where I was once quick to criticize and run, finding tolerance where there was once judgment—this is sacred.

I have pretty much given up blaming you for anything and recognize our deep connection which I have overlooked in the past because it was blocked with fear, shame, anger, and guilt. To nurture our connection, to release blame, and not give into the ego and fear—this is sacred.

As I write this ending to our journey, I am struck with the awareness that I will likely experience your death one day. It is now clear to me that the sacredness of our relationship will not stop at your death, nor will it stop at mine. At some level our relationship will live in my daughters. My deepest hope is that my daughters will have the depth of feeling toward me that I feel toward you in this moment. If that occurs, all the mistakes I make as a father will fade into the mist of the past.

I hope that you live for years to come and my daughters are raised knowing you. But it would be okay for you to die. I feel clean with you. I am not holding onto any guilt or blame.

When you do pass, I hope I can be there. I would like to hold your head with the tenderness and love that you have had in your heart for me. The moment you die I would like to kiss your forehead and send you to God. As your soul leaves your body the last words I will say to you are, *"Thank you for being my father. I love you, I forgive you, I release you."*

When we both die, this book will continue to live and for this I am very proud. I cannot think of a greater message to leave than this: the father and son relationship is sacred. *The connection between father and son is so powerful that it will not rest in repression. Healing the relationship with your father/son is a doorway to life and freedom. Healing is not only possible, it is a necessity for peace.*

With Respect

I honor you, my father,
by recognizing the sacredness of our relationship
and offering you my deepest commitments:
I will strive to be genuine with you;
I will do my best to never run from the power of our
  relationship;
I will do my best to be accessible to you;
I will love you;
I will value forgiveness;
I will see us as teachers and students to each other.

Love, your son
Lee

Dear Lee,

As I read over your last letter to me, your heartfelt thoughts moved me more deeply than I have words to describe. After I had finished reading what you had written, many of my own thoughts and feelings about my dad came bubbling up from the depths of my soul. Even though he is dead, I found myself wanting to write Dad a letter, just as you had written to me. I wanted to tell him about some of the thoughts you and I have been able to share with each other and how they have brought our hearts together in a way that even a year ago we never thought possible.

Lee, there is much I want to tell you directly about what your willingness to do this work together has meant to me. But first I would like to share with you the letter I wrote my dad. Through the writing of that letter, which I am sure became possible for me because of the work you and I have done together, I was able to share my disappointments and joys as his son, and to feel a sense of completion that I had not previously experienced. It occurs to me that other fathers, by writing a letter or poem to their deceased fathers, might find it helpful in their healing process.

Dear Dad,

One of the many unexpected joys I have received in writing this book with Lee is coming closer to you than I ever thought possible.

I am writing this to you as if you were actually alive, sitting here with me, and it doesn't seem like a fantasy to me. In many, many glorious ways I know your presence is actually here with me, right now, right this very moment.

Although it may seem strange to you—and it feels embarrassingly weird and immature to me—there is still a little kid inside of me that misses you, even though I am 70 years old.

I am filled with contradictions. For example, I hate the smell of cigarettes, yet I miss the smell of your body and your cigarette smell. I miss your hugs and your humming and whistling. I miss your softness and above all I miss your gentleness.

I remember you did not like talking about yourself. I never really knew what you were thinking. I remember making up my mind that when I became a father I would identify with your good traits but not your weak ones. I tried very hard to do that, but I was not successful and ended up being angry at you for that.

At last I think I am learning not to feel guilty when my behavior is not perfect. I seem to be very slow at learning what self-acceptance is all about. I am also beginning to learn the value of forgiving others and myself.

I remember one Sunday we spent three hours trying to find

a lion's farm in Los Angeles, only to find later that the farm was in Chicago. I remember Mom ridiculing you, and Les and Art too, and finally I joined in. I am truly sorry, Dad, for any pain I caused you. What is interesting and revealing as I look back at my life, are the many times I put myself in situations where I was ridiculed. Was I just trying to join you, Dad?

Sometimes I didn't think you felt worthy of being loved. I think that for a long time I fell into that trap, too. Today I feel most fortunate indeed, to be able to love myself, to give love, and to receive it too. I don't think I could possibly be loved more by my wife, Diane, my sons, or my family at the Center for Attitudinal Healing. I am truly blessed.

You worked so hard and were so serious, I just don't think you were able to let yourself have very much fun and enjoyment. Perhaps you were still stuck with all that guilt your parents instilled in you. I became angry and blamed you when I found I followed in your footsteps.

There were many times when I wanted you to be different. You did not meet my expectations. Dad, I ask for your forgiveness in expecting you to be perfect. The kid I was back then wanted you to be perfect. I did not honor or accept your humanness.

During the last years of your life, I finally realized that to be gentle, which you were, is a sign of the highest strength. You actually were teaching me this all the time, and I didn't know it.

I am so grateful that you lived long enough to get to know and love your grandsons, Greg and Lee, and for giving them the opportunity to feel your love, and for them to experience love for you. Dad, too many kids today don't get a chance to experience, or even get to know their fathers, let alone their grandfathers. It was such a joy for me to see them love you so openly and tenderly and to see the same love returned to them.

When you died I thought we were complete with each other. I felt I had shared my love with you, and you with me, and that there was nothing we had not said.

I look back at my life with you and I can tell you honestly that I would not have wanted anything to be different. I now know that each event, whether it was pleasant or not, was a lesson I needed for my own growth.

I don't think I told you enough how much I admired the way you handled your blindness during your last years. I also want to thank you, Dad, for teaching me not to make assumptions. I will never forget when, a few years before you died, I decided I would teach you how to meditate. You seemed to spend so much time looking into space. I thought I would teach you how to do something useful during that time.

I was such a slow learner. I still laugh at myself, because that day I found that you had been meditating, in your own way, for most of your life.

I thank you for taking me to the wrestling matches on Thursday nights. Even as a small kid, I didn't like going to places where people were hurting each other. I also thought it was all fake. You always disagreed and were firm in your belief that the matches were all legitimate. I liked going with you anyway, just to spend time with you alone, and I liked the popcorn and the peanuts you bought me. I still like popcorn and peanuts very much. Maybe it is because it reminds me of those times we spent together.

I know you wanted one of your three sons to take over the date store. When Les went to college to become a chemist and Art decided to become an ophthalmologist, all your focus fell on me to follow in your footsteps. I don't believe I ever told you how painful it was for me to disappoint you. I so much wanted to please you. I may be wrong, but I felt it was a sorrow you took to your grave. I hope I am wrong, that you let go of that a long, long time ago.

*It still seems so difficult to put what I feel into words. When I
meditate and pray, I feel your presence and your light. I want you
to know that the hurt past has been released. I have forgiven you
and myself and can see now that there's really nothing to forgive.*

*I feel only your kindness, tenderness, and loving gentleness.
Thank you for being you. Thank you for being my father.*

Dad, I love you with all my heart, now and always.

> *Your loving son,*
> *Jerry*

I want you to know, Lee, that writing this book with you has
been one of the most important experiences of my life. About
halfway through it became clear to me that it was not really
important for anyone else to read it. What was most important was you and me helping each other with the inner healing that was so necessary for each of us.

There have been peaks of joy and valleys of pain for me.
In no way did I realize that the pain would be so great—or
the joy! There have been a number of times when the pain
became so gigantic, I wondered if I had made a mistake in
attempting to open old wounds. I am so happy and grateful
that we both persevered, faced the pain, and went through
and beyond it.

At the beginning I wondered if we would both be flexible enough to get through the rough edges of areas where
we might disagree. Though there was often the old temptation to walk on eggs with you, I chose to always be direct.
Sometimes we ended up disagreeing and having to work
through our different perceptions. I am grateful that your
overall reaction to me throughout the writing of the book
has been open, loving, honest, flexible, and non-attached.
Without your patience and love I'm not sure I would have
made it through.

It has been a wonderful experience for me to be able to speak to you several times a week and, at times, every day. As our communications progressed, I felt a deepening of your love and vulnerability. As a father, I have never thought that I made it easy on you and Greg, and your perseverance in healing our relationship has been deeply helpful and meaningful to me personally.

I too am aware that relationships are not all hearts and flowers and we may very well have temptations in the future to judge and misinterpret each other. I do feel comfortable that each of us has a faith and trust in the power of love and the positive intentions of love that each of us have for one another. Like you, I feel I have shared my heart with you completely.

I think many people might have thrown this entire project in the garbage when faced with the challenges you have been facing in the last year. I have admired the enormous amount of time you have been spending with your kids. I am amazed you have been able to concentrate at the same time on your practice and the emotional job of writing a book with me. I am sure that it is no accident we were writing this book at this time. It has given me another chance, another opportunity, to be nourishing and non-judgmental with you during this time in your life. Thanks for trusting me enough to share with me so intimately.

Writing this book with you has brought me closer to my own father and has brought me closer to God. I feel ever so strongly that God has been with us every step of our journey. I do feel that we have done our best to step aside and let God lead the way. In the process of working with you, I too, have experienced the sacredness of our relationship.

I was moved the other day to write a poem titled, "Frozen River." Writing this book with you has allowed me to see how I and so many other fathers have imposed on others our own blocks to love by hiding our fears and tears. Hopefully, this poem shows us how free we can become when we choose to let go of all of our fears and give everything to our Higher Power.

Frozen River

Unexpressed tears of our childhood,
when frozen in time,
hide our tears and fears as they travel
beneath the ice of our daily existence.
The depth of our despair at feeling abandoned,
remains hidden with the feelings of loneliness
and being left alone to struggle
with the feelings of being unloved
and being unlovable.

When rivers of emotions
become like the frozen river
within fathers and sons,
there is a great tendency to be stone-faced,
have rigid bodies, be tight-assed,
to hide our fearful emotions
from ourselves and others.

The sun begins to shine
and the river begins its spring thaw.
Tears begin to flow
when we own and honor our own emotions,
when we feel our anger
and experience the free flow of our tears
upon being heard
and acknowledged.

The miracle of inner peace and love occurs
when we choose to flow with the river,
when we lose our rigidity
and learn to accept
the curves and bends
the river of life presents to us.

When we learn it is possible
to be honest about our emotions
without dumping on the other person,
that attachments to the hurtful past
do not bring us inner peace and happiness,
we can choose not to be victims,
take responsibility for our own emotions,
and no longer play the game of guilt and blame.
When we forgive ourselves and others
for our own misperceptions,
we open the door to God
and our own healing.

Healing is a letting-go process,
no longer interpreting
each others' words or behavior,
no longer trying to control others
and make them fit into a mold of our own liking.
It is letting go and giving,
absolutely and completely,
everything to God.

Healing is a decision
to live in the forever "now,"
no longer standing in the cold darkness,
immobilized by the frozen river
of our own making.

Healing is the decision to accept
the sacredness of love
and the never-ending light of the sun
that continues to shine in us and upon us
and to choose to constantly give the essence
of the love and light we are to others.

Lee, there have been many times when I felt I had lost you, like when I divorced your mom. When I found out about your drug addiction, I felt I had lost you. I now feel we have found each other. I pray and hope and believe that we will be able to continue to share the sacredness of love with all others on our pathway to the home we have never really left.

I thank you for reaching out and finding your lost father. I embrace you, my son, now and always, with everlasting, never-ending love and gratefulness.

Love,
Dad

Going Further

As we came to the end of writing this book, we felt that many readers would find the following notes helpful. They are aimed at starting to address some of the key issues that men encounter when they make the decision to look for ways to heal their father–son relationships. We have found in our workshops that these simple exercises are ways to focus one's attention and open the doors to the kind of healing we have attempted to describe in these pages.

Symptoms of the Fearful Little Boy in the Adult Male

1. Many men need instant gratification when operating from their fearful little boy. For example, if you want a new car right now, you'll tend to go out and buy one right now, regardless of consequences.

2. Some men become workaholics and are rarely at home with their wives and children. They tend to define the job of parenting as their wives' responsibility.

3. As bosses, their workers are more apt to fear or pity them than to respect them.

4. Based on their parents' relationship, many men grow up not believing in equality in relationships. This is particularly evident in relationships with women. They may be promiscuous and allow double standards for themselves but not for others.

5. Men with the fearful little boy inside may have a deep-seated, unrecognized fear of other men. These men have few or no male friends with whom they would be free to share their inner feelings. They rarely share their feelings and look upon men who do as weak.

6. Men with the fearful little boy inside love and devote a great deal of time to competitive sports. But if someone were to ask them about the personal life of someone they have been playing tennis with for years, they would not have a clue. They would think it a ridiculous question.

7. Men with the fearful little boy inside exhibit rage and anger in a continued rebellion against an authoritarian father. As a result, they become just like the father.

8. A boy who has been abandoned by his father and over-protected by his mother may become a man who looks to women for continued mothering. He will also become afraid of the male world.

9. Boys with weak fathers may become men who always try to be the man their father was never able to be. This man will probably have little sense of self and will rely on aggressive and controlling behavior to get him through life.

10. Boys with absent fathers and domineering, controlling mothers may become men who are afraid of themselves and look to women to tell them what to do.

11. Boys with successful, though absent or abusive fathers may grow up to be men who unconsciously devote their

lives to being different from their fathers, while at the same time trying to equal their father's powerful image.

12. Men who did not have present, emotionally available fathers will likely have a difficult time establishing deep and trusting relationships as grown men.

13. Wounded boys can become men who often act in child-like ways with their spouses and children. They have an unspoken expectation that their wife will mother them whenever they need it. This is often an attempt to duplicate their one close relationship: Mom. Unfortunately, when these men have children of their own, they often compete with them for the mother's affection.

14. Many sons are under-protected and over-punished. The future is viewed as uncertain and the world feels unsafe. Death is never talked about. Fear of aging, death, and punishment may preoccupy much of their existence.

15. Fearful little boys with critical, physically abusive and controlling fathers become men who hide from each other. They become afraid to share their inner lives, inner thoughts, and the tenderness of their hearts. Eventually they hide these even from themselves. They can become either submissive or very manipulative. They are frequently very clever at, and take great pride in, outfoxing their number-one enemy: authority.

Finding Our Fathers

We suggest the following list of questions as a place to begin in getting to know your father.

1. What was your father's childhood like? Find out what you can from whoever might help. How did your father's father relate to him?

2. What did your grandfather teach your dad about expressing feelings? What did the culture of your father's era teach him about men expressing feelings?

3. What was your father's expectations of how you would handle emotional pain and joy? How did he handle emotional pain and joy?

4. Have you been a threat to your father? How has there been any competition?

5. How did/does your father relate to other men?

6. If you asked your dad what are the three most important things about being a man, what would he say? If you asked him what three things he detests in "weak men," what would he say? Would any of his answers have anything to do with expressing feelings?

If you never knew your father, use your imagination. Let your imagination go wild and answer the questions above.

After spending some time answering these questions, allow yourself to redefine for yourself how you want to express your inner life. Answer the following questions, then talk with another man about your answers.

1. How do you want to deal with the pain and joys of life?

2. What do you feel are the five most important aspects of being a man? Be sure to address, in some way, dealing with feelings. Which of these five do you need the most work with? How can you begin to develop these aspects more?

3. How do you want to relate to other men?

Beliefs That Block the Expression of Negative Feelings

1. If I express the anger I feel toward my father, it will hurt him. It is better to suffer than be responsible for the suffering of others.

2. People who are angry are out of control. One should never let themselves be angry.

3. When I saw my father angry, people got hurt. I never want to hurt anybody like that.

4. My father is more powerful than me. If I express my anger he will overpower me.

5. Anger is humiliating. As a kid, every time I got angry my father would put me down by saying things like, "What do you have to be upset about? Look at all you have compared to others."

6. People leave if you get angry. Sometimes they leave emotionally, sometimes physically. My (Jerry) father used to say to me, "Children are to be seen but not heard." If I ever said anything that my dad didn't want me to, he would punish me and then not talk to me for a long time. Although he didn't leave physically, he did emotionally.

7. Being angry is an open invitation to be attacked. Keep your mouth shut and you won't be bothered.

8. Anger and aggression are the same. They are lower emotions that an intellectual person should not have.

9. God can punish me for something, but it is not okay to be mad at God.

10. Anger should be taken out on myself (internalized), because I am usually to blame. My father always blamed me for whatever was wrong.

In reading this list, note that the man who explodes in anger is not necessarily expressing what is really going on. Rage often prevents us from expressing what is really going on in our hearts.

Annotated Bibliography and Suggested Reading

Men's Issues

Ackerman, Dr. Robert J. *Silent Sons: A Book for and About Men.* (New York: Fireside/Simon & Schuster, 1993) An examination of the psychology of surviving a dysfunctional family from a male perspective—refreshingly honest and upbeat.

Allen, Marvin with Jo Robinson. *In the Company of Men: A New Approach to Healing for Husbands, Fathers, and Friends.* (New York: Random House, 1993) A significant, therapeutic contribution to men's healing. Underscored by the author's personal story.

Bly, Robert. *Iron John: A Book About Men.* (New York: Vintage, 1990) The most influential book written about the new vision of what it means to be a man. Without the contribution of this noted poet there might not be a discussion of men's issues today.

Bly, Robert. *A Little Book on the Human Shadow.* Edited by William Booth. (San Francisco: Harper & Row, 1988) Jung's idea of "the shadow" made accessible through poetry and commentary in this concise book based on the author's public readings.

Bly, Robert, James Hillman, and Michael Meade, eds. *The Rag and Bone Shop of the Heart: Poems for Men.* (New York: HarperPerennial, 1992) A lively collection of more than 400 poems used in the editors' workshops. An excellent introduction to the power of poetry for both men and women.

Diamond, Jed. *The Warrior's Journey Home: Healing Men, Healing the Planet.* (Oakland, CA: New Harbinger, 1994) An ambitious work of personal vision and planetary responsibility that champions authentic male stewardship in partnership with the feminine.

Gilmore, David D. *Manhood in the Making: Cultural Concepts of Masculinity.* (New Haven, CT & London: Yale University Press, 1990) An important, myth-shattering cross-cultural study broadening the definition of masculinity.

Glennon, Will. *Fathering: Strengthening Connection With Your Children No Matter Where You Are.* (Berkeley, CA: Conari, 1995) A divorced father challenges men to remain an essential part of their children's lives.

Gurian, Michael. *The Prince and the King: Healing the Father-Son Wound—A Guided Journey of Initiation.* (New York: Jeremy P. Tarcher/Perigee, 1992) Healing the father–son relationship through the use of storytelling and meditation.

Hillman, James. *A Blue Fire.* Edited by Thomas Moore. (New York: HarperPerennial, 1991) An intellectual feast by one the most iconoclastic and original psychological thinkers of our time.

Johnson, Robert A. *The Fisher King and the Handless Maiden: Understanding the Wounded Feeling Function in Masculine and Feminine Psychology.* (San Francisco: HarperSan

Francisco, 1993) This noted Jungian analyst has made a career of exploring the masculine and feminine in a body of work acclaimed for its brevity and clarity. Johnson opens the reader to the world of relationship psychology enriched by tales of wisdom from mythology and folklore.

————.*He: Understanding Masculine Psychology.* (New York: HarperPerennial, 1974)

————. *Inner Work: Using Dreams and Active Imagination for Personal Growth.* (San Francisco: HarperSan Francisco, 1986)

————. *Lying with the Heavenly Woman: Understanding and Integrating the Feminine Archetypes in Men's Lives.* (San Francisco: HarperSan Francisco, 1994)

————. *Owning Your Own Shadow: Understanding the Dark Side of the Psyche.* (San Francisco: HarperSan Francisco, 1991)

————. *She: Understanding Feminine Psychology.* (New York: HarperPerennial, 1976)

————. *Transformation: Understanding the Three Levels of Masculine Consciousness.* (San Francisco: HarperSan Francisco, 1991)

————.*We: Understanding the Psychology of Romantic Love.* (San Francisco: Harper & Row, 1983)

Kauth, Bill. *A Circle of Men: The Original Manual for Men's Support Groups.* (New York: St. Martin's Press, 1992) A guidebook for forming men's groups.

Keyes, Ralph, ed. *Sons and Fathers: A Book of Men's Writing.* (New York: HarperPerennial, 1992) Father and son reflections from various writers.

Kimbrell, Andrew. *The Masculine Mystique: The Politics of Masculinity.* (New York: Ballantine Books, 1995) A practical work decrying the societal status quo and calling on men to revolutionize the values of the corporate culture.

Kipnis, Aaron. *Knights Without Armor: A Practical Guide for Men in Quest of Masculine Soul.* (New York: Jeremy P. Tarcher/Perigee, 1991) A mature revisioning of masculinity by a psychologist who offers a broadly based work that expands and complements other works in the field while stressing the profound need for men's healing in all aspects of their lives.

Kritsberg, Wayne, John Lee, and Shepherd Bliss. *A Quiet Strength: Meditations on the Masculine Soul.* (New York: Bantam Books, 1994) A selection of daily readings for men on the path of healing and wholeness.

Lee, John. *The Flying Boy: Healing the Wounded Man.* (Deerfield Beach, FL: Health Communications, 1987) Coming to terms with relationship healing and the search for intimacy.

Lee, John. *At My Father's Wedding: Men Coming to Terms with their Fathers and Themselves.* (New York: Bantam, 1991) A sincere statement of a son's hunger for healing with his father. Passionate and informed, this book will ring true for many men.

Levinson, Daniel J. *The Seasons of a Man's Life.* (New York: Ballantine Books, 1978) The seminal study of the male life span, also the basis for Gail Sheehy's *Passages.*

Meade, Michael. *Men and the Water of Life: Initiation and the Tempering of Men.* (San Francisco: HarperSan Francisco, 1993) An epic account through myth and storytelling of men's (and women's) struggles to come to terms with some of the deepest issues—violence, passion, love, creativity, generativity, and race—that face our culture and world.

Moore, Robert and Douglas Gillette. *King, Warrior, Magician, Lover: Rediscovering the Archetypes of the Mature Masculine.* (New York: HarperCollins, 1990) The primer for understanding Jungian archetypal psychology in masculine development.

Nerburn, Kent. *Letters to My Son: A Father's Wisdom on Manhood, Women, Life and Love.* (San Rafael, CA: New World Library, 1994) One of the clearest and most beautiful statements of a father's love for his son.

Osherson, Samuel. *The Passions of Fatherhood.* (New York: Fawcett Columbine, 1995) Celebrating the wonders of being a father.

———. *Wrestling with Love: How Men Struggle with Intimacy.* (New York: Fawcett Columbine, 1992) Difficulties men have in finding and maintaining intimate relationships.

Pedersen, Anne and Peggy O'Mara, eds. *Being A Father: Family, Work, and Self.* (Santa Fe, NM: John Muir Publications, 1990) Essays on many aspects of being a father.

Pirsig, Robert M. *Zen and the Art of Motorcycle Maintenance: An Inquiry into Values.* (New York: Bantam Books, 1974) A profound philosophical book that works on many different levels. Read it for its extraordinary father and son story.

Powell, Joanna, ed. *Things I Should Have Said to My Father: Poignant, Funny and Unforgettable Remembrances from Memorable Sons.* (New York: Avon Books, 1994) A collection of short writings on fathers by their famous sons.

Shapiro, Jerrold Lee. *The Measure of a Man: Becoming the Father You Wish Your Father Had Been.* (New York: Perigee, 1993) A ground breaking study of how a man's relationship with his father influences his parenting style. An eye-opening book for both men and women.

Thompson, Keith, ed. *To Be a Man: In Search of the Deep Masculine.* (New York: Jeremy P. Tarcher/Perigee, 1991) Leading edge thinkers, classic writers, poets and philosophers explore notions of manhood in this provocative collection.

Psychology/Relationships

Bennett, Hal Zina. *The Lens of Perception.* (Berkeley, CA: Celestial Arts, 1994) A look at human consciousness and making sense of the world by viewing it spiritually.

Bradshaw, John. *Creating Love: The Next Great Stage of Growth.* (New York: Bantam Books, 1992) Relationship healing by ending destructive patterns of behavior learned early in life.

——. *Family Secrets: What You Don't Know Can Hurt You.* (New York: Bantam, 1995) A compelling look at the "dark secrets" found in every family and the powerful psychological hold they retain over us.

——. *Homecoming: Reclaiming and Championing Your Inner Child.* (New York: Bantam Books, 1990) A step-by-step program for healing and liberating the inner child.

Brown, Lyn Mikel and Carol Gilligan. *Meeting at the Crossroads: The Landmark Book About the Turning Points in Girls' and Women's Lives.* (New York: Ballantine Books, 1992) One of the first reports detailing society's mistreatment of adolescent girls. Important for men who wish to better understand the women in their lives, especially fathers raising girls.

Dyer, Wayne W. *Your Sacred Self: Making the Decision to Be Free.* (New York: HarperCollins, 1995) In Dyer's latest work, the popular psychologist and speaker continues his move from traditional psychology to deep spirituality as the path toward wholeness.

Estés, Clarissa Pinkola. *Women Who Run With the Wolves: Myths and Stories of the Wild Woman Archetype.* (New York: Ballantine Books, 1992) Men who want to understand the "wild" nature in women should read this powerful, popular work of women's depth psychology.

Gray, John. *Men Are from Mars, Women Are from Venus: A Practical Guide for Improving Communication and Getting What You Want in Your Relationships.* (New York: HarperCollins, 1992) Gray's works offer accessible and useful techniques for improving gender communication and relationship skills.

————. *Men, Women and Relationships: Making Peace with the Opposite Sex.* (Hillsboro, OR: Beyond Words Publishing, 1993)

————. *What You Feel You Can Heal: A Guide for Enriching.* (Mill Valley, CA: Heart Publishing, 1984)

Houston, Jean. *The Possible Human: A Course in Enhancing Your Physical, Mental and Creative Abilities.* (Los Angeles: Jeremy P. Tarcher/Houghton Mifflin, 1982) Mind expansion exercises by the visionary teacher/thinker.

————. *The Search for the Beloved: Journeys in Mythology and Sacred Psychology.* (New York: Jeremy P. Tarcher/Putnam, 1987) Spiritual yearning and the soul's hunger for the Divine become the path of transformation in this workbook based on the teachings and exercises developed by the author.

Jampolsky, Gerald G. *Change Your Mind, Change Your Life.* (New York: Bantam, 1993) Techniques for personal and planetary change by altering the way we think.

————. *Love is Letting Go of Fear.* (Berkeley, CA: Celestial Arts, 1979) A small book that takes a gentle, light-hearted approach to some of life's deepest issues.

————. *One Person Can Make A Difference: Ordinary People Doing Extraordinary Things.* (New York: Bantam, 1990) An uplifting message about our unlimited potential.

————. *Out of Darkness Into the Light: A Journey of Inner Healing.* (New York: Bantam, 1989) The author's own story of inner struggle and personal transformation.

————. *Teach Only Love: The Seven Principles of Attitudinal Healing.* (New York: Bantam, 1983) Deepening our experience of the unique and transforming power of love.

————. and Diane V. Cirincione. *Love is the Answer: Creating Positive Relationships.* (New York: Bantam Books, 1991) A married couple's advice on achieving lasting peace and real love in relationships.

————. and Diane V. Cirincione. *Me First and the Gimme Gimmes.* (Deerfield Beach, FL: Health Communications, 1991) An illustrated book for children on sharing.

————. and Diane V. Cirincione. *Wake-Up Calls.* (Carson, CA: Hay House, 1992) Thoughts on achieving peace through practical spirituality.

————. with Patricia Hopkins and William N. Thetford. *Good-Bye to Guilt.* (New York: Bantam Books, 1991) The releasing of false guilt as the necessary step in the forgiveness of one's own life and others.

Jampolsky, Lee. *Healing the Addictive Mind: Freeing Yourself from Addictive Patterns and Relationships.* (Berkeley, CA: Celestial Arts, 1991) The first exploration of changing addictive behavior patterns by applying the principles found in *A Course in Miracles.*

————. *The Art of Trust: Healing Your Heart and Opening Your Mind.* (Berkeley, CA: Celestial Arts, 1994) Presents a six-step process for developing trust within ourselves, which in turn enriches our relationships.

Keen, Sam. *Fire in the Belly: On Being a Man.* (New York: Bantam Books, 1991) A profound and powerful reimagining of manhood. One of the most influential books written about the modern male. Keen's works, listed below, form one of the clearest statements of living in psychological and spiritual balance in today's world.

———. *Hymns To An Unknown God.* (New York: Bantam Books, 1994)

———. *Inward Bound: Exploring the Geography of Your Emotions.* (New York: Bantam Books, 1980)

———. *The Passionate Life: Stages of Loving.* (San Francisco: HarperSan Francisco, 1992)

———. *To a Dancing God: Notes of a Spiritual Traveler.* (San Francisco: Harper & Row, 1990)

Lee, John. *Facing the Fire: Experiencing and Expressing Anger Appropriately.* (New York: Bantam Books, 1993) Confronting the reality of anger in our lives and finding methods for its authentic, non-destructive expression and release.

Moore, Thomas. *Care of the Soul: A Guide for Cultivating Depth and Sacredness in Everyday Life.* (New York: HarperPerennial, 1992) *Care of the Soul* and *Soul Mates* are companion volumes that serve as handbooks for adding spirituality, depth and meaning to modern-day life by nurturing the soul.

———. *Soul Mates: Honoring the Mysteries of Love and Relationship.* (New York: HarperPerennial, 1994) Soul-centered psychology on the relationship journey.

Prather, Hugh. *I Touch the Earth, the Earth Touches Me.* (New York: Doubleday, 1972) The second book in a series of diaries by Prather beginning with *Notes to Myself.*

———. *Notes on How to Live in the World ... And Still Be Happy.* (New York: Doubleday, 1986) Exercises and advice on sane living in a seemingly insane world.

————. *Notes on Love and Courage.* (New York: Doubleday, 1977) Third in the series of Prather's diaries, beginning with *Notes to Myself.*

————. *Notes to Myself: My Struggle to Become A Person.* (New York: Bantam, 1970) A human potential classic and publishing phenomenon that became the starting point for many spiritual seekers over the last two decades. The first in a series of highly personal diaries, *Notes to Myself* is as honest, authentic, and life-affirming as it was when first published twenty years ago.

————. *There Is A Place Where You Are Not Alone.* (New York: Doubleday, 1980) Finding that we are never alone in the world when we learn to be truly helpful to others.

————. *A Book of Games: A Course in Spiritual Play.* (New York: Doubleday, 1981) Games meant to teach and bring about real peace of mind.

————. *The Quiet Answer.* (New York: Doubleday, 1982) Gentle wisdom for returning to the heart of silence and the peace of God.

————. and Gayle Prather. *A Book for Couples.* (New York: Doubleday, 1988) For twenty years the Prathers have been speaking the language of spiritual transformation. Each book they've written together offers a gentle invitation to reexperience the world through acceptance, forgiveness, and love.

————. and Gayle Prather. *I Will Never Leave You: How Couples Can Achieve the Power of Lasting Love.* (New York: Bantam Books, 1995) Advocacy and advice on long-term commitments by a couple who have been doing marriage counseling for many years.

————. and Gayle Prather. *Notes to Each Other.* (New York: Bantam, 1990) The Prathers write back and forth about the joys and difficulties of being a couple in the style of *Notes to Myself.*

————. and Gayle Prather. *Parables from Other Planets.* (New York: Bantam, 1982) Stories meant to startle, entertain, inform, and enlighten.

Sheehy, Gail. *New Passages: Mapping Your Life Across Time.* (New York: Random House, 1995) An optimistic look at the potential quality of life possible in later years, noting the shifts that occur in male and female dynamics over time.

Tannen, Deborah. *You Just Don't Understand: Women and Men in Conversation.* (New York: Ballantine Books, 1990) How men and women hear each other and often misunderstand each other.

Spirituality

A Course in Miracles. (Mill Valley, CA: Foundation for Inner Peace, 1975) A three-volume set of books, Christian in statement, that deals with universal spiritual themes.

Fields, Rick. *Chop Wood, Carry Water: A Guide to Finding Spiritual Fulfillment in Everyday Life.* (Los Angeles: Jeremy P. Tarcher/Houghton Mifflin, 1984) A handbook for the inner journey containing ancient wisdom for contemporary seekers.

Kabat-Zinn, Jon. *Wherever You Go There You Are: Mindfulness Meditation in Everyday Life.* (New York: Hyperion, 1994) Using the Buddhist principle of mindfulness to attain physical and mental health.

Krishnamurti, J. *The Book of Life: Daily Meditations with Krishnamurti.* (San Francisco: HarperSan Francisco, 1995) A varied compendium of the spiritual teacher's short, insightful essays.

Nhat Hanh, Thich. *Peace Is Every Step: The Path of Mindfulness in Everyday Life*. (New York: Bantam Books, 1991) A simple explanation of Zen Buddhist techniques of meditation and awareness by the pioneer of engaged Buddhism.

Peck, M. Scott. *The Road Less Traveled: A New Psychology of Love, Traditional Values, and Spiritual Growth*. (New York: Touchstone/Simon & Schuster, 1978) The popular, now-classic study of living a life based on spiritual values.

Schwartz, Tony. *What Really Matters: Searching for Wisdom in America*. (New York: Bantam Books, 1995) A *New York Times* journalist's conversations with leading psychologists, philosophers, physicians and scientists.

Sell, Emily Hilburn, ed. *The Spirit of Loving: Reflections on Love and Relationship by Writers, Psychotherapists, and Spiritual Teachers*. (Boston: Shambhala, 1995) An inspiring collection of quotations celebrating love in all its dimensions.

Vaughan, Frances and Roger Walsh. *Gift of Peace*. (New York: Jeremy P. Tarcher/Putnam, 1986) Abridged writings arranged in thematic and poetic form from *A Course in Miracles*—serves as an excellent introduction to the larger work.

———. *Accept this Gift*. (New York: Jeremy P. Tarcher/Putnam, 1992) More abridged writings from *A Course in Miracles*.

Williamson, Marianne. *A Return to Love: Reflections on the Principles of A Course in Miracles*. (New York: HarperPerennial, 1992) An exploration of modern themes and issues with a spiritual focus based on the popular talks and lectures of the author.

For those readers interested in learning more about lectures, workshops, tapes, and other books by the authors, write to:

The Center for Attitudinal Healing
33 Buchanan Street
Sausalito, California 94965